Cold Blooded Killers

A guide to the deadliest and most dangerous animals on the planet!

By

Peter Elliott
© 2014 Peter Elliott

KINDRED
SOUNDS

I couldn't have made this book without the valuable contribution from my trusty researchers Sachi and Kenji, two of the world's most passionate aficionados of deadly animals.

This book is dedicated to all the rodents that gave their lives so that we might be able to know the LD50 ratings of various venoms. Because of your sacrifice, we know how many of you will die per drop of a particular venom. This has allowed us to…well, actually not much. But hey, at least we know that 50% of you will die when given 0.002mg/kg of Geographic Cone Snail venom. Who would have thought?

Contents

Introduction

You know you are writing an interesting book when you constantly have to breathlessly run through the house to find your wife so you can blurt out *"Did you know that the male Black Widow spider tries to avoid being eaten by the female, however the closely related Redback Spider will actually place himself in front of her mouthparts so she will eat him and therefore contribute nutrition towards his babies?"*

This book has been fascinating to research from start to finish, however after finishing I noticed that one or two animals were dead boring. So I cut them out. If these animals subsequently demonstrate the requisite level of intrigue, I will add them in when I create the second edition. So if you read this book, throw it to the ground in contempt as you drop to your knees screaming *"You omitted Hippos - Africa's deadliest animal!"* this is the reason why. However, that being said, if you read this and find a glaring omission, please send me an email so I can look into including it. Use my provision of an email address (or lack thereof) as a tacit indication of my actual willingness to follow through with this offer.

Anyway, I digress.

The deadly animals in this book can be roughly broken into the following general categories -

1. Venomous (they bite or sting you, injecting venom)

2. Poisonous (they poison you if you eat them or come into contact with them in some way)

3. Animals that attack and eat you.

This book does not aim to be an encyclopaedic reference for these various deadly animals, but rather, a digest version with all the boring bits taken out. The aim is for pure entertainment with a sprinkling of education.

What does "deadly" actually mean?

First things first - We need to define "deadly" and establish how we are to measure this "deadliness" we speak of.

Defining "deadly" for a shark is actually quite easy. How many people does it attack? How many people does it kill? However, for venomous creatures it is often problematic giving a simple answer to this question. Firstly, we need to have a clear definition what we mean when we say "deadliest", as this could mean -

- **Most people killed** - Since records began or recently?
- **Most toxic venom** - Given an equal amount of venom, which animal could kill the most people?
- **Most toxic bite** - This would need to factor in the toxicity of the venom and the amount of venom injected.
- **Most aggressive?** Certain animals will bite you if you look at them sideways, whereas others, you could pull their pants down, give them a wedgie and make suggestive comments regarding their girlfriends and they won't do a thing.

In the interests of clarity, we should consider "deadly" to refer to what happens if this creature envenomates or poisons a human and "dangerous" to refer to how many people the animal has killed. So, to use the Inland Taipan as an example again, it would be considered highly deadly (due to the toxicity of its venom) but not particularly dangerous (due to its isolated habitat).

Secondly, there is a lot of variability between different records. One lot of tests could generate one result and another lot could generate completely different numbers. The perfect example of this would be the Belcher's Sea Snake which, according to some is the most venomous snake on earth and according to others, only moderately potent. So even if we agree on the LD50 (Don't worry – I will get to the meaning of LD50 in a moment) value for a particular species, this value itself could change depending on where the animal bites another animal or a human. And then we could get a completely different result between mice and humans. Mice are usually used for LD50 tests; however our metabolism is different to rodents, so certain animals (particularly snakes, who are specialized rodent hunters) could have completely different levels of "deadliness" depending on the animal being bitten.

This problem becomes especially evident if we look at the Australian Inland Taipan, which has, drop for drop the most potent venom of any snake. Fortunately for Australians, the Inland Taipan lives out in the middle of nowhere and has a shy disposition, which means that no-one has ever died from an Inland Taipan bite (that we know of for certain). In contrast, Africa's Black Mamba has less toxic venom than the Inland Taipan (although still extremely toxic compared to most snakes) but is a notorious cantankerous and comes into regular contact with people, resulting in thousands of fatalities every year.

LD50 - Median lethal dose - The cruel gold-standard for measuring the toxicity of venom and poison

So, for the purposes of this book, we will consider LD50 to be the best yardstick of deadliness for any venomous creatures henceforth. The LD50 value (or median lethal dose) is the lethal dose ("LD") for half ("50 %") of the test subjects used. So, if an animal's LD50 value is 0.1 mg/kg, it will take 0.1 mg per kilogram of body mass to kill 50% of the test animals. Fortunately, due to the inherent cruelty associated with this testing methodology, it is now being phased out in favour of methods that don't require the sacrifice of any mice. However, the greatest amount of data on venom toxicity is still in the LD50 format, so that is the format we will reference in this book.

We must also take into consideration the amount (yield) of venom injected in each bite. The yield is significantly more problematic to pin down considering all the differing ways that animals achieve envenomation or toxin delivery. For example, you have snakes and spiders that inject venom via fangs and animals like Poison Dart Frogs that don't bite but instead secrete toxins through their skin to deter predators. This in itself can be problematic due to the lack of reliable yield data for many venomous creatures.

Another source of confusion is the route of delivery the animal uses. So the same venom will have dramatically different LD50 values depending on whether the venom is delivered *subcutaneously* (SC), *intravenously* (IV) or *intramuscularly* (IM).

Even if we just concentrate on LD50 values, there is no clear consensus regarding the exact LD50 value for particular animals due to discrepancies in the test results. So where I have found a range of values I have averaged out to reach a rough consensus. Internet forums the world over are full of passionately debated threads regarding comparative LD50 values and measures of deadliness so please don't take it that we consider this list the last word in venom toxicity.

The World's Most Toxic Creatures

Based on LD50 values and amount of venom injected, the most deadly animals in the world are - (Note - the lower the LD50 value, the more toxic the venom) (Yield only listed for those creatures with reliable data available)

Poison Dart Frog	0.002 mg/kg	N/A
Geographic Cone Snail	0.004 mg/kg	N/A
Blue Ringed Octopus	0.008 mg/kg	N/A
Puffer Fish	0.008 mg/kg	N/A
Box Jellyfish	0.020 mg/kg	N/A
Inland taipan -	0.025 mg/kg	44 mg
Dubois' sea snake	0.044 mg/kg	0.7 mg
Black mamba	0.050 mg/kg	75 mg
Eastern brown -	0.053 mg/kg	4 mg
Boomslang	0.057 mg/kg	4.5 mg
Yellow-bellied sea snake	0.067 mg/kg	2.5 mg
Coastal taipan -	0.099 mg/kg	120 mg
Hook-nosed sea snake	0.112 mg/kg	8.5 mg
Brazilian Wandering Spider	0.120 mg/kg	N/A
Coral snake	0.120 mg/kg	6 mg
Puff adder	0.140 mg/kg	200 mg
Gaboon Viper	0.140 mg/kg	450 mg
Mojave rattlesnake	0.150 mg/kg	100 mg
Beaked sea snake	0.150 mg/kg	8.5 mg
Tiger snake	0.150 mg/kg	80 mg
Malayan blue krait	0.150 mg/kg	N/A
Sydney Funnel Web	0.160 mg/kg	2 mg
Philippine Cobra	0.200 mg/kg	300 mg
Deathstalker Scorpion	0.250 mg/kg	N/A
Saw-Scaled viper	0.300 mg/kg	N/A
Common India Krait	0.365 mg/kg	10 mg
Stonefish	0.370 mg/kg	N/A
Death adder	0.450 mg/kg	65 mg
Cobra	0.565 mg/kg	169 mg
Tiger rattlesnake	0.600 mg/kg	6 mg
Russel's Viper	0.750 mg/kg	180 mg
Stonefish	0.800 mg/kg	N/A
Black Widow Spider	0.900 mg/kg	N/A
Redback Spider	0.900 mg/kg	2 mg
King Cobra -	1.800 mg/kg	421 mg

Things to note

Before we move on, it is probably important to point out the difference between venomous and poisonous. A venomous creature harms you when it bites you. A poisonous creature harms you when you bite it. Or, to put it another way, venom is offensive (used to secure and eat prey) while poison is defensive (used by an animal to deter other animals from trying to eat it). So now you can get as illogically angry as I do when I see a site on the internet listing "the world's most poisonous snakes".

Another distinction that is important we make, is that venom can be delivered by a bite (as in a spider or a snake) or a sting (as in a jellyfish).

The venom and poison used by each creature is rarely a single toxin, but more commonly a cocktail of different proteins, enzymes and other toxins, each with a unique function. In general, venom is one of the following types -

Hemotoxins - Destroys red blood cells, stops clotting or causes tissue damage.

Neurotoxins - Damages aspects of the nervous system by disrupting neurochemistry and nerve transmission

Myotoxins - Damages muscles

Cardiotoxins - Damages the heart

So, without any further ado, let's move on to the first group of animals and the only ones in this book that do all their damage without any need for poison or venom.

Sharks

Largely thanks to Steven Spielberg's 1975 movie *Jaws*, few animals possess the ability to strike fear into humans than the ocean's most successful apex predator - the shark. This is despite that fact that few sharks are even remotely dangerous to humans. In fact, out of the hundreds of different species of shark, only three are associated with a significant number of attacks on humans - the Bull Shark, the Tiger Shark and the grand-daddy of today's nightmare-inducing sharks - the Great White Shark (or White Pointer).

A good indication of the success of any particular animal is how long it has roamed (or swam or flown) the earth and the oceans. Measured by this standard, sharks amply demonstrate their long-term success on earth, with ancestors of today's sharks being recorded more than 400 million years back in time. Sharks even pre-date the dinosaurs.

These amazing creatures not only saw the rise and demise of the dinosaurs, but ancestors of today's great whites were genuinely the stuff of nightmares. The truly frightening Megalodon was three times the size of today's largest great whites and had the strongest bite force (how hard it chomps down) of any creature that has ever lived. Try your best not to imagine a great white shark that is 18 metres long. Ever since I first imagined meeting one of these in the ocean, I have to wear brown underpants and cannot sleep alone.

Despite the regular attacks on humans, scientists believe the majority of attacks are due to cases of mistaken identity. The most common scenario occurs when a shark mistakes a surfer for a seal when attacking from below, or when someone is attacked in murky water.

One thing we should point out is that, even though we have elected to only classify the Great White, Bull and Tiger Sharks as "deadly", there are many other sharks with confirmed attacks on humans the led to a fatality. However, in general, these attacks are isolated and more often than not due to either provocation or a case of mistaken identity. So, in the interests of completeness, the other sharks which have been implicated in fatal attacks on humans are - the Bronze Whaler,

Galapogos Shark, Oceanic White Tip, Dusky, Sand Tiger, Shortfin Mako, and the Blue Shark. One surprising omission is the little known salmon shark, which is a relative of the Great White and a seriously scary looking shark. I am surprised to hear it has never killed a human - probably because it hunts in such freezing cold water up near Alaska.

The other point which needs to be made is that, while we have listed three sharks as "deadly", the number of people killed by sharks is astoundingly low. Sharks have killed less than 569 people since records began in the 16th century! In comparison, in the same period, mosquitoes have killed hundreds of millions of people and continue to kill more than a million people each year.

Sharks - *scary?* Yes. *Deadly?* Not particularly.

Did you know?

- Many sharks are endangered due to poaching (for shark-fin soup) or accidentally becoming tangled in fishing nets
- A shark's skeleton is made of cartilage - similar to the substance which is between your joints
- There are almost 500 species of sharks, ranging from the 15-20cm long lantern shark to the 12 metre long whale shark (Don't worry - whale sharks are no danger to you - they are filter-feeders, living off tiny marine creatures)
- Sharks are often referred to as "apex predators", which means that they are at the top of the food chain. Sharks, like other apex predators in the ocean, are sometimes dangerous to eat because of high levels of mercury. This is because mercury concentrates each additional step up the food chain. Sharks, tuna and sailfish can have particularly large concentrations of mercury in their flesh. Mercury is a highly toxic heavy metal which is particularly dangerous for the human brain.
- Unlike humans, sharks can continue to replace lost teeth throughout their lives. From an evolutionary perspective, this makes perfect sense. Grandpa can get false teeth to help him continue to enjoy steaks into his twilight years - sharks don't have this luxury, so if they couldn't replace their teeth, they could die after losing them to

misadventure.

- The majority of all sharks need to constantly swim in order to breath, as the movement through the water enables them to absorb oxygen through their gills. *So how do they sleep?* I hear you ask. They are essentially able to swim while asleep.
- Some sharks, when turned upside down, enter a state known as "tonic immobility", where they appear to be asleep or hypnotised. I enter a similar state at Andre Rieu concerts. So next time you are attacked by a great white, carefully turn the shark over while singing something soothing. If this doesn't work, scream loudly and evacuate the contents of your stomach so you can confuse the animal.
- Sharks have unique electroreceptor organs called the *ampullae of Lorenzini*, which enables it to detect electrical signals given off by potential prey. These ampullae look like small gel sacs when examined by cross-section. This unique organ gives the shark the most powerful ability to detect electrical signals of any animal known.
- The young of certain shark species are known for the unusual practice of *oophagy*, which is where the first baby shark to hatch will then eat all the unhatched eggs. The sand tiger shark takes this sibling rivalry one step further by eating its siblings after they have hatched. This further ensures that survival of the fittest continues to strengthen sharks as a species. There are obviously no poor sickly sharks with a club foot and asthma - they were all eaten.
- The fastest shark is the Short-fin Mako, which can hit top speed of 50km/h over short distances. To put this in perspective, this is around the average speed that a car travels around town.
- Sharks kill around 5-10 people worldwide each year. During the same period, humans will kill, on average, around 100 million sharks.
- Australia is by far the shark attack and shark fatality capital of the world, with almost 700 attacks and 220 deaths on record. Within Australia, Western Australia is the shark-attack capital of Australia - due mainly to a large population of Great Whites.
- There are several reasons why so many people end up surviving a shark attack. Firstly, sharks are known to often take *test bites* as they work out whether something is worth eating. Many attacks are believed

to be test bites where the shark didn't like what it tasted and allows the person to escape. Secondly, sharks are known to ambush prey, taking a large initial bite with the intention of immobilising the prey, whereupon the shark can wait until the prey either dies or is incapacitated. It is thought that sharks use this strategy to prevent unnecessary injury to themselves. Why risk your prey injuring you as it thrashes around (like a seal tusk for example), when you can sit back and wait it out? However, humans are almost unique in their ability to escape out of the water and out of harm's way.

- If you wish to minimise your chances of attack, make sure you -
  - Avoid swimming at dusk or dawn or when the conditions are overcast
  - Avoid murky water (particularly for Bull Sharks)
  - Don't swim if you are bleeding
  - Don't splash around too much
  - Don't swim near populations of animals that sharks traditionally hunt - such as seals.
- Alternatively, if you wish to maximise your chances of being eaten, you could head to Seal Island in South Africa, cut your feet on a craggy rock and head out for a relaxing dusk swim with those gorgeous cape fur seals. You may want to get your affairs in order beforehand.

Great White Shark (*Carcharodon carcharias*)

In terms of fear-factor, no other ocean creature comes close to the Great White in the minds of people. While their ferocious reputation is deserved, they are hardly the mindless eating machines that they are often portrayed as. They are highly intelligent, with complex behaviour and fascinating physiology. However, when your nickname is *white death*, you tend to get off on the wrong foot with people, no matter what you do.

The Great White is the largest of all predatory sharks, growing to around 6.5 metres long (although larger specimens have been reported, fisherman are notorious for their exaggerations).

The reputation of the great white in modern times was unquestionably amplified by the huge box office hit *Jaws*, which premiered way back in 1975. After Jaws became popular, there was a whole generation of beach goers who were too scared to enter the water, despite the fact that they were nowhere near typical Great White hunting grounds.

Did you know?

- The Great White is the last surviving member of the genus *carcharodon*

and is a descendent of the truly frightening 18 metre Megalodon.
- The Great White is the ultimate apex predator among sharks, with no known predators of its own…except…
- The Killer Whale! Did you know that Great Whites are virtually helpless against Killer Whales? A fascinating phenomenon has been witnessed several times and even captured on video. Killer Whales can apparently ram themselves into Great Whites, knocking the shark on its side or back, triggering *tonic immobility* (see introduction for more on this). Once immobilised, the killer whale then proceeds to deliberately eat the shark's liver while it is still alive. The Great White is then left to die. What I find most amazing about this is the fact that the Killer Whales appear to know the exact location of the shark's liver and are only interested in this organ, discarding everything else. Killer Whales are notorious for eating only certain parts of some of the larger animals they kill (they will often only eat the lower jaw of whale calves they kill). Killer Whales are up there with wasps and hornets as the most brutal animals on the planet.
- Interestingly, after the two confirmed incidences of a Killer Whale killing a Great White was that shortly after the shark was killed, all the tagged sharks in the area fled the California coast where the attack occurred! Some of these sharks didn't stop until they reached Hawaii! Great Whites appear to be genuinely afraid of Killer Whales.
- Great whites can, over short distances, reach speeds of around 30mph (45-50km/h). The Short-fin Mako is slightly quicker and can maintain their speed over longer distances.
- Great whites are famous for their reputed ability to smell a drop of blood in the ocean, however this tends to get exaggerated and surrounded in myth. Many people erroneously believe that if they have a cut on their body somewhere, sharks from kilometres away will suddenly descend on them. A slightly more accurate assessment is that a great white can smell a single drop of blood in a whole Olympic-sized swimming pool. An impressive feat nonetheless!
- Great whites have been around for at least 16 million years, making them an extremely successful predator.
- Due to their unique ability regenerate heat inside their bodies, Great

Whites can tolerate large extremes in water temperature. This is the reason why they are found in so many parts of the world, including the USA, Mexico and parts of South America. The greatest concentrations of Great Whites however are in Australia and South Africa. In terms of specific locations, the greatest number of sharks are found at Dyer Island (South Africa), South West-WA (Australia), South Australia and Guadalupe Island (Mexico).

- Great Whites migrate over huge distances. One shark was tagged and was then seen to travel around 20,000km between South Africa and Australia in nine months.

- Great Whites utilise a type of camouflage called *countershading* (or *Thayer's Law*), where the top half is dark and the bottom half is white. This means, when prey looks down, the dark shading on the great white will provide an element of camouflage. Likewise, if prey looks up, the white underside will be camouflaged against the brighter surface of the water.

- There has always been considerable debate as to the size of the largest great white ever caught. For many years it was believed to have been a shark landed in Port Fairy, Australia, in the 1870s, which was apparently measured to be 11 metres long! However, later this was proved to be inaccurate when the jaws of this particular specimen were measured, leading to a more realistic estimate of 5 metres. I am guessing that the shark was originally measured at 5 metres in length, however each time the fisherman told the story to his buddies, the length gradually increased.

- The largest Great Whites that were measured by reliable means was a 6 metre behemoth landed off Western Australia and an even bigger 6.1 metre specimen caught off Prince Edward Island in Canada. Apart from these, there are quite a few other specimens where the fishermen involved claim lengths approaching 7 metres; however none of these were measured to acceptable standards.

- The Great White's electromagnetic sense (via the *ampullae of Lorenzini*, like many other sharks) is extremely sensitive and can even sense the electricity given off by your heart-beat, if you were close enough. So if a five metre Great White is bearing down on you, make sure you keep your heart rate slow and gentle.

- The Great White will also occasionally raise its eyes above the surface of the water in a practice called *spyhopping*. Scientists are not sure whether they do this to visualise prey or to pick up particular scents. Either way, I don't like to imagine this scenario if I am swimming. The idea of a great white rising out of the water right next to me to look me in the eye doesn't bear thinking about.
- The Great Whites at South Africa's Seal Island have developed a particularly terrifying behaviour known as *breaching*. A Great White will wait in the deep until the shadow of a fur seal passes overhead. Then, it will rocket towards the surface so fast that the shark's entire body flies out of the water. Surprisingly, the fur seals are not completely defenceless. A curious behavioural adaptation was captured by a documentary film crew. The seal has an agility advantage over the Great White and is smart enough to take advantage of this. In this particular incident, the shark missed the seal on the first attempt and was trying to then catch it as it swam around. This is where the seal did something interesting. It followed the shark around, sticking on its tail! Because of the seal's agility advantage, as long as it stayed on the tail of the Great White (i.e. - away from the other, more dangerous, end), the shark was unable to catch it. Eventually the shark appeared to make a calculation that its efforts were best focused on a new ambush and it gave up, leaving the seal to swim safely back to the island
- Great Whites have one of the most mysterious reproduction habits of any creature, with little known about how and where they reproduce. The only evidence is a poorly shot, shaky webcam clip which has been floating around the internet. For research purposes I checked it out but was only able to make out a dorsal fin. It wasn't worth the $5.99 charged to my credit card.
- Great Whites appear to not prefer human beings because humans have a much higher bone to fat ratio than typical great white prey such as seals. As I have a bone to fat ratio roughly approximating a seal, I tend to exercise considerable caution while swimming. Most attacks on humans are therefore thought to be cases of mistaken identity, as our silhouettes can appear seal-like from below. Just for a moment now, imagine that

you are swimming and decide to peer down into the depths below you and you see a great white hurtling up towards you. I will leave you with that thought.

- Great Whites also occasionally attack boats. It is believed that they may become confused by electrical signals given off by the boat's engine or electronics. Similarly and on a rather more petrifying level, they have also been known to knock kayakers into the water. Thankfully (and surprisingly) these incidents do not typically end in an attack.

- Unfortunately, Great Whites do not handle captivity well - hence the complete absence of any specimens at your local aquarium. For many years, any great white held in captivity soon died. Since then there have been some isolated successes. Particularly the Monterey Bay Aquarium in California has had some success keeping Great Whites in one of its large tanks. The best result to date was a specimen they were able to keep alive for around nine months before being released into the ocean.

Bull Shark (*Carcharhinus leucas*)

Each year the Bull Shark and the tiger shark are neck and neck for attacks and fatalities. The Bull Shark is particularly dangerous because it loves to hang around where humans tend to congregate - in shallow waters, rivers, estuaries and channels. Not only this, but Bull Sharks love to hunt in murky waters, which can lead to humans being bitten in cases of mistaken identity. The Bull Shark is also involved in a large number of attacks simply because of its strong constitution (it can handle a wide range of water conditions) and consequent wide distribution. This is reflected in the large geographical area across which Bull Shark attacks are spread.

In fact, some experts believe that many older shark attacks (before advanced bite measuring techniques allowed scientists to identify the shark responsible for a particular attack) which were initially attributed to Great Whites, were actually Bull Sharks. Therefore, it's possible that over the last century, many more Bull Shark attacks may have actually occurred than they are credited with.

Did you know?

- Bull Sharks get their name from their stocky, solid build. They are like the rugby players of the ocean. So while they only really get to 3.5 metres as a maximum size, they can weigh as much as 320kg.
- The Bull Shark is famous for its ability to tolerate fresh water. Bull Sharks have been tracked hundreds of miles inland, as they are able to live in rivers and estuaries. A Bull Shark was once found all the way up the Mississippi river in Illinois!
- In Africa, the Bull Shark is known as the Zambezi shark and is responsible for many fatalities each year.
- The Bull Shark has the strongest bite force of any fish or shark in the ocean - greater than the great white. Scientists believe that this bite force is linked to their freshwater habitat and perhaps their love of turtles (they need to be able to crunch through the shell).

Tiger Shark (*Galeocerdo cuvier*)

The final instalment of our deadly trifecta of sharks is dedicated to the Tiger Shark - another shark you should probably avoid while swimming. The Tiger Shark is, along with the Bull Shark, a member of the *carcharhinidae* family (or *Requiem* shark). They are called *Tiger Shark*s because of their tiger-like dark stripes.

Tiger Sharks are less tolerant of cold water and are therefore more likely to be found in tropical waters across the globe. Sometimes they are even found in much colder regions as they are able to follow the *gulf stream*, taking advantage of the relatively warm water (the *gulf stream* is a warm water current which flows north from Florida, up the east coast of the USA and into the Atlantic ocean, keeping ocean temperatures warmer than would usually be expected based on the latitude).

The Tiger Shark is the second largest (behind the Great White) of the predatory sharks (filter feeders like the whale shark and the basking shark are considerably larger), growing to around 4 metres in length. The largest specimen ever recorded was a big, bouncing 5.5 metre unit caught off Australia (*Note - after reading this whole guide, I think you will realise that we are unlikely to receive any funding from Tourism Australia).*

Did you know?

- The Tiger Shark has eyes specially evolved for hunting at night and in low light conditions. Their eyes are able to pick up isolated photons of light that other animals would not be able to detect
- Unlike humans, Tiger Sharks are negatively buoyant, which means that they naturally sink downwards (unlike humans, who float upwards).
- Tiger Sharks are famous for eating anything, hence the stories of finding motor vehicle license plates in their stomachs. Among other things, sharks eat - dolphins, turtles, fish, jellyfish, other sharks, crustaceans and sea snakes.
- Tiger Sharks have also been known to eat dogs, cats, horses and goats! I don't know which is more surprising - that Tiger Sharks eat cats or that there is actually a cat that will willingly enter the ocean. I feel genuinely sorry for a cat that is taken by a Tiger Shark. I imagine that it took years to work up the courage to swim in the ocean in the first place. Then, for the cat to get eaten is particularly tragic.
- Dolphins are generally petrified of Tiger Sharks and therefore tend to avoid areas where they are found in high numbers.
- The Tiger Shark is classified as *near threatened* due to the fact that there are a large number of morons who target them for the fins. The practice of shark finning involves slicing off the shark's fin and then throwing the shark back in the ocean to die a slow death. These fins are then used to make shark fin soup which rich Chinese people order to show others how affluent they are, despite the fact that the shark fin adds little to the flavour of the soup. Shark fin soup apparently tastes like a mixture of chicken stock and suffering. This is one of the reasons why Tiger Shark populations have dropped by as much as 90% in the last century.
- Also exacerbating the drop in the Tiger Shark population was the widespread culling of Tiger Sharks in Hawaii from the 1950s to the 1970s, where almost 5000 Tiger Sharks were killed to protect the tourism industry there. Ironically the number of attacks stayed steady

since then.

- Since the 16th century, less than 30 people have been killed by Tiger Sharks. So despite their fearsome reputation, they barely even qualify as "deadly".

Snakes

To give you an idea of just how frightening snakes are to not just humans but other mammals as well, it's worth noting that our brains come "pre-installed" with a primordial fear of serpents.

If you are walking through the jungle or similar terrain and you suddenly see a long thin shape on the ground, a part of your brain called the *amygdala* will put you on high alert, possibly causing you to jump back and emit a small, girlish squeal like I imagine I would. Then, moments later, another part of your brain will realise that it was just a piece of rope or a stick and you will then relax.

This is not just a learned fear either. Scientists have found that baby primates raised without any other primate parental figures will have a natural fear of snakes. It appears to be written into our programming.

And generally for good reason too. Even with the advent of antivenin for most snake bites, snakes still kill an astounding number of people each year. Conservative estimates put this number at tens of thousands per year, with most of the deaths concentrated in South Asia, Southeast Asia, and sub-Saharan Africa, where the victims are either isolated or without access to antivenin. Some estimates put the number of people killed in India alone at more than 30,000!

Snakes kill prey by either constriction or envenomation. Constricting species (such as Pythons and Anacondas) will squeeze prey tight until the hapless animal takes a breath. When the animal breathes out, the snake squeezes tighter so the animal can't take an in breath. Envenomation involves biting the victim and injecting venom through its fangs which act like hypodermic needles.

Like most animals, the vast majority of snakes are harmless to humans and among those that can cause injury, a smaller number again can accurately be called "deadly". Snakes that are either harmless or kill animals by constriction we refer to as "boring" and won't be mentioning again in this book.

Despite the fearsome reputation of snakes, they are usually rather shy creatures and will only bite if provoked or accidentally disturbed. Many will also *dry-bite*, where they bite but do not inject venom, as they may quite rightly realise that venom is wasted on large animals such as humans, who they would be unable to eat. Only certain types of snakes (like King Cobras) have the specialized muscle required for controlling venom delivery, enabling them to *dry-bite*.

Venomous snakes belong in two separate families -

> *Elapids* – Cobras, Kraits, Mambas and all Sea Snakes.
> *Viperids* – Vipers, Rattlesnakes, Copperheads and Cottonmouths

Snake Venom

Snakes produce their venom in modified salivary glands and store it is special ducts, where it can then be injected into the victim via fangs that operate like a hypodermic needle.

Broadly speaking, there are a range of different toxins that snakes use to incapacitate and kill their prey -

Neurotoxins - Used by the snake to cause paralysis by acting on the central nervous system

Myotoxins - Used to damage muscle cells to achieve paralysis by different means to neurotoxins

Hemotoxins - Used by the snake to kill the animal by causing internal bleeding or preventing clotting

Nephrotoxins - Used to kill the animal by causing kidney failure

Cardiotoxins - Used to kill the animal by causing cardiac arrest and cardiac arrythmias.

Necrotoxins - Cause tissue death at the site of the bite, incapacitating the prey

Each snake can have both a mix of the same type of toxin (for example - Tiger Snake venom contains around 6 different neurotoxins) and a mix of toxins.

Based on LD50 values and reported fatalities, the most toxic, most deadly and the most dangerous snakes are -

Inland Taipan -	0.025 mg/kg	44 mg
Dubois' Sea Snake	0.044 mg/kg	0.7 mg
Black Mamba	0.050 mg/kg	75 mg
Eastern Brown -	0.053 mg/kg	4 mg
Boomslang	0.057 mg/kg	4.5 mg
Yellow-bellied Sea Snake	0.067 mg/kg	2.5 mg
Coastal Taipan -	0.099 mg/kg	120 mg
Hook-nosed Sea Snake	0.112 mg/kg	8.5 mg
Coral Snake	0.120 mg/kg	6 mg
Russell's Viper -	0.133 mg/kg	180 mg

However the list changes slightly when we also take into consideration venom yield -

Gaboon Viper -	0.140 mg/kg 450 mg
Inland Taipan -	0.025 mg/kg 44 mg
Black Mamba	0.050 mg/kg 75 mg
Puff Adder	0.140 mg/kg 200 mg
Coastal Taipan -	0.099 mg/kg 120 mg
Mojave Tatttlesnake	0.150 mg/kg 100 mg
Tiger Snake -	0.150 mg/kg 80 mg
Boomslang -	0.057 mg/kg 4.5 mg
Russell's Viper -	0.133 mg/kg 180 mg
Philipine Cobra -	0.200 mg/kg 100 mg

Then, if we look at the deadliest snakes based on the number of people killed each year, we get an almost entirely different list -

Saw-Scaled Viper - up to 50,000 per year
Puff Adder - up to 32,000 per year
Russel's Viper - up to 25,000 per year
Carpet Viper - up to 20,000 per year
Indian Cobra - up to 15,000 per year
Common Krait - up to 10,000 per year

Before I proceed, a few disclaimers regarding this information -

- LD50 values are massively variable, meaning you either need to cherry pick the data to find the most reputable source or you need to average out the data. Because of this, everyone's Top 10 can look a little different - particularly for those snakes coming in between 7 and 10 on the list. The list can also look different based on someone's acceptance of sea snake values - particularly the Belcher's Sea Snake which some sources list as the most potent venom on the planet and others believe to be only moderately toxic.
- Some LD50 values are based on subcutaneous injection (SC), others based on intravenous (IV) and others based on intramuscular (IM). Based on the nature of a snake envenomation, my sense is that, in general, subcutaneous values would be the most appropriate.
- LD50 values are mice-specific. Quite rightly, many people are critical of the LD50 system for this reason as humans respond differently to different toxins than mice do. Remember, snakes are evolved to prey on rodents.

Note that these numbers are notoriously unreliable due to inconsistent reporting from isolated and remote communities in India and Africa. For example, estimates on total number of snakebite deaths each year range from as low as 15,000 to as high as 90,000.

As you can see, the most venomous snakes are nowhere to be found on the list of the most dangerous snakes, which is why many people (perhaps quite rightly) believe that LD50 values are purely academic. If you get bitten by a deadly snake, what does it matter whether there is enough venom to kill 20 people or only one person? As long as a particular snake packs enough venom to kill a single person quickly with each attack, the snakes that are located in A) Densely populated areas and B) Third world countries (lack of access to antivenin, isolated from the nearest hospital, tend to sleep on the ground) will always quite rightly be considered the deadliest. In contrast, despite the fact that between 1000 and 3000 people each year get bitten by a snake in Australia, fatalities are exceedingly rare. This is because of the world-class health system and wide availability of antivenin.

Did you know?

- Snakes produce venom in modified salivary glands that sit behind their eyes.
- The snake's forked tongue enables it to sense prey in 3D. Microscopic scent molecules hit the snake's tongue, enabling it to locate the prey. It does this by then transferring the scent molecules into an organ inside its mouth called the *Jacobsen's Organ*, which then processes the information and sends it to the brain.
- Snakes have no way of chewing, so they have to eat their prey whole, however their flexible jaw design means they can eat prey bigger than their own heads.
- Certain sea snakes can breathe a little through their skin. This enables them to spend longer periods underwater hunting prey
- The largest snake to have ever lived was the *Titanoboa*, which slithered the earth around 60 million years ago
- In some parts of the world, snakes have a unique foe - the Mongoose. Mongooses prey on snakes, using their amazing agility and immunity to snake venom to deadly effect.
- Sea snakes have a lung that runs almost the entire length of their body and the ends of their tails have often evolved into a flattened shape which acts like a flipper or a paddle.
- A sea snake on the shore should never be picked up as they will sometimes "play dead" if they have been left stranded by tidal movements, waiting until the rising tide takes them back out to sea. If

you disturb a sea snake that was playing dead, they can be surprisingly cranky!

- All of the venomous snakes in Australia (and in the waters surrounding Australia) are elapids - there are no vipers in this area.

Inland Taipan (*Oxyuranus microlepidotus*)

The Inland Taipan is perhaps the perfect embodiment of the dichotomy between "dangerous" and "deadly", as it possesses by far the most potent venom of any snake, yet is responsible for no confirmed deaths. The lack of death toll is primarily a function of its environment – it is located literally in the middle of nowhere, out in the Australian outback. Humans just don't have many opportunities to encounter one of these snakes in its natural environment. However the temperament of the Inland Taipan is also a factor, as it is renowned as a placid snake which is shy and will usually either slither away from humans, or stand its ground and tolerate our company without striking. The only exceptions are when it is cornered or handled aggressively. However even then it will provide ample signals that it is not happy and would like you to leave it alone. If, after being provided due warning, you decided to accost the world's most venomous snake, you were probably going to die by misadventure anyway by using a hairdryer in the bath or falling into a log chipper.

A single bite from an Inland Taipan has the ability to kill around 100 human adults. This begs the question – Why does a snake that hunts small mammals need to be so outrageously over-engineered? There is no proven single answer, however there is a fairly strong theory. Researchers have noticed that laboratory mice are significantly weaker to the Inland Taipan's venom compared to the rodents that the snake typically encounters in the wild. It has been hypothesised that Inland Taipans are in an "evolutionary arms race" with their prey. As their prey gradually develops a degree of immunity to the venom, the snake itself is under evolutionary pressures to keep up with increasingly potent venom. However there may be other forces at work too. Inland Taipans live in harsh, barren environments where energy is valued and protected. Perhaps these snakes cannot afford to produce lavish quantities of moderately potent venom (remember, most snake cherish their venom and will spare it where possible – suggesting a great degree of physiological effort goes into its manufacture). Perhaps they have therefore needed to produce something that will do the job without needing large quantities of venom. This idea is supported by the relatively small yield per bite, compared to other snakes such as the cobras or rattlesnakes. Lastly, the venom potency may reflect the need to immobilise prey quickly so that they do not have the ability to get far from the snake – a similar concept to the Cone Snail mentioned later in the book. This idea is backed up by the fact that neurotoxins which cause paralysis form an important part of the venom.

Assuming you were foolhardy enough or unlucky enough to be bitten by an Inland Taipan, the last thirty minutes or so of your life would not be pleasant. On top of all the usual neurotoxin-related problems like vomiting and convulsions, the Inland Taipan's venom is also myotoxic, breaking down muscle tissue. You would know about this if you (for some bizarre reason) decided to urinate (not the best use of your last 30 minutes in my opinion to be honest) because your urine would turn reddish-brown as your dissolving muscles get sent to your kidneys. The fun doesn't stop there however, as there is also a cheeky little hemotoxin that rears its head, leading to massive internal bleeding and death.

Did you know?

- The nickname of this snake (the "Fierce Snake") creates the false impression that we are talking about an aggressive character, however in this case "fierce" refers to the frightening potency of the venom, not the disposition of the snake.
- One thing that struck me as odd while researching the Inland Taipan is that we have a good description of what it does when threatened and forced to strike, however we have no record of anyone being bitten. So all I can assume is that we have provoked it from a safe distance (or with some kind of protective wear) to see what happened. I wonder who drew the short straw at the animal enclosure that day.

Cobras (*Naja*)

    With their distinctive hood that expands when threatened, cobras are perhaps the most iconic and recognisable of all snakes. They are perhaps most closely associated with the Indian practice of snake charming - a practice possible due to the cobra's ability to raise itself high up off the ground (like the Black Mamba).

    Cobras are typically found in hot tropical regions of Asia, Africa and the Sub-Continent. There are a large number of different types of Cobra, however the most dangerous are the Phillipine Cobra, Forest Cobra, King Cobra, Cape Cobra and the Indian Cobra. Many cobras are able to deliver a fatal bite, injecting varying amount of mainly neurotoxic (but also cardiotoxic for some species) venom. As you saw in the earlier calculation of the deadliest snakes, one of the reasons why cobras are particularly dangerous is that they typically envenomate large quantities of venom when they strike. However there are also many cobras which pose minimal risk to humans.

Did you know?

- There is a type of cobra called the Spitting Cobra which has a unique defence. Any animal that gets too close will have venom shot into their eyes. They don't *inject* venom - they *eject* it. Sometimes as far as 2 metres!
- Cobras form their distinctive hood by spreading out their ribs which are attached to skin flaps.
- Like most snakes, Cobras are not proactively aggressive and will hiss loudly to warn off an aggressor. Bites are seen as a last resort.
- Cobras are in the *elapidea* family which also includes Black Mambas and Taipans.
- The King Cobra is the largest venomous snake in the world, reaching almost 4 metres in length. It is also reputed to be the most intelligent of snakes and loves nothing better than eating other snakes. This makes courtship between two King Cobras particularly fraught. Documentary crews filming King Cobras have witnessed them eating the opposite sex during what appeared to be the lead up to mating. Something suddenly changes and one of them decides they are more hungry than frisky. Assuming mating concludes with both snakes still possessing all their arms, legs and fangs, the female will actually create a nest for her eggs - the only snake in the world that does this.
- While snake charmers appear to be foolhardy, in most cases they either remove the snake's venom sac or render the fangs inactive. The practice of snake charming is, quite rightly, therefore considered cruel. If you visit India, spend your money on someone who deserves it - not a snake charmer.
- The King Cobra is not actually a "true" cobra!

Eastern Brown Snake (*Pseudonaja textilis*)

The Eastern Brown quite rightly deserves its reputation as one of the most deadly snakes in the world. Due to the fact that the Inland Taipan rarely comes into contact with humans and almost never envenomates people, the Eastern Brown should be considered Australia's (if not the world's) deadliest snake based on the strength of the venom.

Eastern Browns are found all up and down the east coast of Australia and is able to tolerate and thrive in a wide range of environments all the way from wet rain-forests to deserts. More problematic however is their habit of entering suburban areas in search of a meal. This is what brings them into contact with people sometimes.

The Eastern Brown's venom consists mainly of neurotoxins and coagulants (the venom makes blood clot). It is a testament to the sheer potency of their venom that they only inject small quantities when they envenomate prey or humans. Fortunately, Eastern Browns are known for using a dry bite initially and then envenomating if this fails to allay their concerns. If bitten, diarrhoea and dizziness will soon start. If left untreated, this can then end in cardiac arrest or kidney failure. Like many neurotoxins, the Eastern Brown's works by blocking the action of the important neurotransmitter *acetylcholine*.

Fortunately, due to the wide availability of antivenin and the first class health system in Australia, deaths are quite rare these days.

Did you know?

- In March 2014 an Australian man named Rod Sommerville was bitten on the hand by an Eastern Brown. As he remembered hearing that panicking only spreads the venom more quickly throughout the body, he decided to relax the only way he knew how - by sitting back and enjoying a cold beer while waiting for paramedics to arrive. He told reporters that if he was going to "cark it", he might as well do so while having his last beer. Despite an allergic reaction to the antivenin, he eventually made a full recovery and is now able to continue enjoying his favourite beverage.
- In another case, an Australian boy came close to perishing after picking up a dead Eastern brown. While playing around with the dead snake, he accidentally pricked his hand with one of the fangs and soon became extremely ill. Eastern brown venom can remain active even after the snake has died or the venom has dried out.

Black Mamba (*Dendroaspis polylepis*)

Despite the fact that other snakes such as the Saw-Scaled Viper kill more people in Africa each year, if there is one snake that can strike fear into the heart of any African it is the Black Mamba. This is due to the fact that not only does it possess one of the strongest venoms in the animal kingdom, it also moves with frightening speed and possesses one of the most disagreeable temperaments of all snakes. Black Mambas clearly have not read the book *How to Win Friends and Influence People* (Perhaps - *How to Kill Friends and Envenomate People*? Sorry, that was terrible). Adding to the fearsome persona is the fact that the Black Mamba is also the longest venomous snake in the world, reaching up to 14 feet in length.

You are possibly wondering why they are known as "Black" Mambas when they are conspicuously brown or olive-coloured. The "Black" part of the name comes from the inside of their mouth which is jet-black. Trust me; you don't want to find this fact out first hand. If you get to see the inside of their mouth, you should take a moment to allow your life to flash before your very eyes.

Despite the fact that they are an aggressive variety of snake, if confronted and they have a means of escape, they will often do so to preserve venom. However if cornered or startled they won't hesitate to strike.

Black Mambas are distributed throughout large parts of Africa, with the greatest concentrations in The Republic of Congo, Kenya, Ethiopia and Somalia.

The Black Mamba's neurotoxic venom is so deadly that often someone will only have 20 minutes to get administered antivenin to prevent death. Left untreated, the fatality rate is 100%.

Did you know?

- One of the other most eye-catching features of Black Mamba behaviour is their ability to lift one-third of their body off the ground, apparently bending the laws of physics. They are therefore unsurprisingly, good climbers, allowing them to hunt baby birds or eggs. Their propensity to spend time in trees leads to many fruit pickers being bitten.
- Another reason why the Black Mamba is so dangerous is that they will often strike several times, sometimes injecting large quantities of venom.
- Just two drops of the Black Mamba's venom can kill a person

Death Adder (*Acanthophis antarcticus*)

Adding to Australia's inordinately long list of deadly snakes is the Death Adder, which is found mainly on the Eastern seaboard of the country, along with parts of Papua New Guinea.

Rather than stalking its prey, the Death Adder is an ambush hunter, lying in wait while camouflaged in leaf litter or scrub. Herein lays the problem for humans, who can accidentally step on or startle a nearly invisible Adder, leading to envenomation. A more mobile and active snake will often flee if they hear a human approaching, however a Death Adder will remain immobile, leading to a greater chance of being stepped on and consequently lashing out.

Did you know?

- Rather than laying eggs, the Death Adder gives birth to live young. However, rather than staying to tend for her young, squealing with joy as they take their first slither, the mother will instantly abandon her young and head off to get on with her life.

- A big problem for the Death Adder (and not to mention, humans too) is the ghastly Cane Toad - an overseas pest that was introduced into Australia as part of the most cock-eyed scheme ever hatched by man. The Cane Toad was brought to Australia to control the Cane Beetle, subsequently turning into an infinitely greater problem than any beetle. As the Cane Toad is poisonous, Death Adders often perish after eating one.
- The Death Adder has one of the fastest strikes of all snakes.

Rattlesnakes (*Crotalus*)

Rattlesnakes are a type of Pit Viper (along with other snakes such as Lanceheads and Eyelash Vipers) found throughout large parts of the Americas (USA, Canada, Central America and South America). Due to their wide distribution and potent venom, the various Rattlesnake varieties are the leading cause of reported snakebite in North America.

Their most distinctive feature is also the one that prevents much of the risk of being bitten. When threatened, a Rattlesnake makes a large sound with its "rattle" that sits at the end of its tail.

There are a range of different Rattlesnakes, from the Western Diamondback Rattlesnake (which is responsible for the most number of attacks on humans) to the Mojave Rattlesnake (which possesses the most dangerous strike due to a combination of potent venom and high yield) to the Tiger Rattlesnake (which possesses the most potent venom of all the Rattlesnakes).

Like the Death Adder, the Rattlesnake is an ambush hunter, waiting for prey to wander into its strike zone. The Rattlesnake will envenomate its prey and wait for it to wander off and die. The snake will track the prey, keeping its distance until it is sure the animal is dead. Many snakes do this to avoid being injured by struggling prey.

The Rattlesnake's venom is quite complex and, depending on the variety, can be hemotoxic (interrupting blood clotting and destroying red blood cells), neurotoxic (affecting the neurotransmitter acetylcholine) and can even cause localized tissue necrosis. Despite the wide range of action, the venom is only moderately potent and consequently there are few deaths each year. This means that although up to 8000 people are bitten annually, typically less than 5 people will die. If antivenin is administered within a reasonable time after envenomation, survival rates are close to 100%. Symptoms of the bite can include pain, oedema (swelling), muscle weakness, panic and nausea. Left untreated, heart failure is also possible.

Did you know?

- The stomach acid and digestive enzymes in the Rattlesnake are so powerful; it can fully digest even small bones!
- As with other Pit Vipers, the Rattlesnake has two heat-sensing pits near its eyes that it uses to sense warm-blooded prey
    - STUFF OF NIGHTMARES WARNING! If you cut the head off a Rattlesnake, it can remain conscious and RETAIN THE ABILITY TO BITE YOU for up to an hour. No, I am not making this up.

Coastal Taipan (*Oxyuranus scutellatus*)

Poor old Coastal Taipan. In any other country this snake would feature prominently in the nightmares of any person unfortunate enough to place themselves within biting distance. Unfortunately, when you live in the same part of the world as the Inland Taipan and the Eastern Brown, you tend to fade into the background. Which is amazing when you consider that this snake possesses one of the most powerful neurotoxic venoms in the world.

If you get bitten by a Coastal Taipan and you don't receive antivenin in time, you have a 100% chance of "carking it", as Queensland's Eastern Brown victim Rod Sommerville would say.

If you are unfortunate enough to be bitten, you will first experience headache, nausea (accompanied by vomiting) and dizziness. If you don't get prompt treatment, this will be followed by convulsions, coma and then death.

Fortunately, like its "Inland" cousin, the Coastal Taipan has a relatively shy and retiring countenance and will almost always try to avoid confrontation with humans.

Did you know?

- The Coastal Taipan can occasionally grow to up to 12 metres in length.
- A man working in thick bushland in Queensland was recently bitten by a Coastal Taipan and reportedly died "almost instantly".

Puff Adder (*Bitis arietans*)

Things don't sound good when a creature's proper name is "Bitis", as is the case with the deadly Puff Adder.

Due to its wide distribution all throughout the African continent, the Puff Adder is responsible for more deaths each year than any other snake on the continent. Other snakes (like the Black Mamba) have more deadly venom, but none kill more people in Africa than this highly successful viper.

Perhaps surprisingly, as well as possessing a moderately potent cytotoxic venom that belies the number of fatalities, the venom of the Puff Adder also acts relatively slowly, giving the victim time to seek treatment. Therefore it comes as no shock to find that virtually all fatalities are due to lack of appropriate medical facilities in poorer areas of Africa. This means that, quite frustratingly, the 30,000 plus deaths each year from Puff Adder bites should be considered preventable with appropriate funding and investment in medical infrastructure. I assume that the millions of potential deaths from more widespread problems in Africa (such as dysentery) get priority over snake antivenin, however it is frustrating nonetheless.

Did you know?

- It is known as the Puff Adder due to its habit of puffing itself up to appear larger when it feels threatened
- The Puff Adder is one of the few snakes that gives birth to live young (not eggs)
- Strangely, young, recently born Puff Adders can be more deadly than adults as they can have poor control over the amount of venom injected when they bite, leading to a much higher dose.

Boomslang (*Dispholidus typus*)

The Boomslang is conspicuous as the only *colubrid* snake that features among the world's deadliest snakes. Snakes in this family tend to be relatively harmless, with the Boomslang a notable exception. All of the other snakes that feature on this list are either *elapids* or *vipers*.

This striking green snake which is native to sub-Saharan Africa, injects its venom via long fangs that sit at the back of the mouth. The venom is also quite different to most of the elapids and vipers, in that it is primarily hemotoxic, interfering with the blood-clotting process. The victim consequently dies of uncontrolled internal bleeding. Fortunately, due to their non-aggressive nature, the Boomslang typically prefers to flee rather than attack. This means that human fatalities are comparatively low compared to other African snakes like the Puff Adder and the Saw-Scaled Viper.

The Boomslang's venom is also notable for its comparatively slow onset of symptoms. This can be a double-edged sword as, while it allows people time to get treated with antivenin, it also can lead to people believing they will be fine and won't require treatment.

Did you know?

- One of the magical potions features in J.K. Rowling's Harry Potter series called for Boomslang skin as one of the key ingredients.
- The name Boomslang means "tree snake" in Afrikaans.

Saw-Scaled Viper (*Echis carinatus*)

If we are to define the "world's deadliest snake" in terms of deaths caused per annum, the Saw-Scaled Viper is the front runner, responsible for up to 50,000 deaths per annum. The large death toll is not due to a particularly potent venom (its venom doesn't make the top ten most venomous snake venoms, drop for drop). The Saw-Scaled Viper kills such a large number of people each year because it is distributed widely throughout the Indian subcontinent, central Asia and the Middle East. This is exacerbated by the fact that it tends to live around people and tends to be found in poorer, third-world countries with limited access to antivenin. Put another way, if this snake lived in Australia, you probably wouldn't even know it existed.

The Saw-Scaled Viper is a member of the *Big Four*, which is a colloquial term for the four snakes that are responsible for the majority of snakebite deaths in India. Other members of the group are the Indian Cobra, the Common Krait and Russel's Viper.

Left untreated, a bite from a Saw-Scaled Viper can lead to internal bleeding and eventually kidney failure.

Did you know?

- The venom of the Saw-Scaled Viper is such a powerful anticoagulant (it stops blood from clotting) that it has been made into a medicine called echistatin.
- The Saw-Scaled Viper is one of the smallest of the venomous snakes on this list, averaging around 45 centimetres in length.
- STUFF OF NIGHTMARES WARNING! The Saw-Scaled Viper is one of the few snakes that will actually pursue you! Most snakes will bite and flee, whereas the Saw-Scaled Viper is known for getting so agitated that, on occasion, it will hunt you down.

Gaboon Viper (*Bitis gabonica*)

Another deadly snake found in sub-Saharan Africa is the Gaboon Viper.

As you saw earlier, while the Gaboon Viper has moderately potent hemotoxic venom, it is the huge venom yield that makes this snake particularly deadly. Delivering this massive payload are the longest fangs of any venomous snake, clocking in at around 5cm in length. They are big snakes too, considered the heaviest of all venomous snakes, reaching upwards of 20kg.

The Gaboon Viper is also quite striking in appearance, with two small horns between the nostrils and skin covered in distinctive patterns.

Fortunately, the Gaboon Viper tends to stay away from humans, preferring to hang out in rainforests, away from major population centres. Just about the only way to get bitten is to accidentally step on one - and even then they may not bite. These incidents tend to occur due to the Gaboon Viper's expertise in camouflage. One of these snakes sitting in leaf litter is virtually invisible.

If you are unlucky enough to get bitten, even if you survive, you are in for a rough afternoon that may feature convulsions and soiling yourself.

Did you know?

- One of the reasons why the Gaboon Viper delivers so much venom in each strike is that it is a "bite and hold" snake. This means that when it bites prey, it holds on to the prey, continuing to inject venom. Most snakes will strike and then withdraw to let the prey die. This helps them avoid being injured by the struggling animal. With the help of its huge fangs, the Gaboon Viper will hold on to the animal until it is dead.
- The Gaboon Viper is a notoriously languid snake, preferring to move around only when it is absolutely necessary. While lying in wait for prey, Gaboon Vipers have been recorded not moving a single muscle for more than two days. This is also one of the reasons why Gaboon Vipers can go an entire year without eating.
- This economy of movement, along with the striking and beautiful markings it possesses, makes the Gaboon Viper a popular pet for snake enthusiasts, who keep them in purpose-built aquariums. And yes, as you may have expected, each year a handful of people are bitten by their pet viper after putting their hand into the glass enclosure. And yes, alcohol is commonly a factor. Morons.

Russell's viper (Daboia russelii)

Another member of the "Big Four" Indian snakes is Russell's viper, a snake responsible for up to 25,000 deaths per year. However, the Russell's viper is not just an Indian snake - it is found all throughout Asia and the Sub-Continent. As with the other snakes that take the most human lives each year, the lethality of this snake is a factor of the venom strength, venom yield, wide geographical distribution, tendency to live near humans and the fact that it is located in primarily third-world countries with relatively poor healthcare infrastructure.

At around an LD50 of 0.133 mg/kg, the hemotoxic venom of the Russell's Viper just misses out on the top ten snakes for venom potency, but when combined with a high yield (average around 180mg), this snake becomes one of the top 10 deadliest. However, where this snake excels is in the damage it can do to a human being even if they are lucky enough to survive the bite. Initially, the Russell's viper bite is known to be exquisitely painful, due in part to the extreme swelling which occurs at the site of the bite. This is then followed by systemic bleeding, evidenced by blood in the urine and mouth. Kidney failure can then eventuate either soon after or even months later (assuming you survive). The Russell's viper venom is also unique in its ability to sometimes destroy your pituitary gland - a vital component of your endocrine (hormonal) system.

Did you know?

- As I have mentioned throughout this book, scientists are studying the venom of various creatures for potential future treatments of various diseases. Because Russell's viper venom is such a powerful modulator of coagulation (blood clotting), it is used for various diagnostic tests looking at blood thinning or blood clotting.
- Russell's viper venom is also being investigated as a potential treatment for the debilitating neurological condition Alzheimer's disease. One fraction (a component of) Russell's viper venom appears to break down the beta amyloid plaque that is associated with this condition.
- The Russell's viper is responsible for more than 90% of all snakebite deaths in Burma. In fact, in most parts of Central and South-East Asia, the Russell's viper is by far the deadliest snake.
- There is a video circulating on the internet (sorry I won't put links here because links tend to die and some may be reading the paperback version) where a drop of Russell's viper venom is dropped into blood in a Petri dish. Within moments the blood clumps into a single mass, showing the powerful coagulant abilities of this venom.

Common Krait (*Bungarus caeruleus*)

Another member of India's "Big Four" is the Common Krait, which is found mainly in the Sub-Continent and as far afield as Nepal and Afghanistan. The Common Krait's neurotoxic venom (0.335 LD50) is only moderately potent; however its tendency to cohabitate with humans and a lack of appropriate treatment in the areas it lives means that it can kill tens of thousands each year.

One of the problems with the Common Krait is that the bite is virtually painless. Many do not even realise that they have been bitten. This can mean that valuable time is lost in seeking treatment. Without administration of antivenin, death by respiratory paralysis can occur within 8 hours. Due to the lack of pain at the time of envenomation and the delay between being bitten and dying, the Common Krait is believed to be responsible for many more deaths than those reported. Victims can literally go to bed feeling fine and never wake up. The best initial sign that you have been bitten by a Common Krait is drooping of the eyelids.

Did you know?

- The Common Krait is easy to identify due to its distinctive white bands.
- One of the most common causes of Common Krait envenomation is sleeping on the ground, as this snake is most active at night so there is more chance of it getting under blankets. There is a theory in India that they like to lick sweat off your skin while you sleep - however this is unproven.

Dubois Sea Snake (*Aipysurus duboisii*)

At around 0.044 mg/kg LD50 value, the Dubois Sea Snake (also known as the Reef Shallows Sea Snake) possesses the second most powerful venom of any snake - just behind the Inland Taipan. However, fortunately, just like the Inland Taipan, the Dubois Sea Snake poses little risk to humans as it has a tiny venom yield and is not found in heavily populated areas.

The world's deadliest sea snake (in terms of venom potency) lives in the warm seas around Papua New Guinea and northern Australia, feeding mainly on various fish and eels.

Did you know?

- Unlike many other sea snakes, the Dubois Sea Snake lives entirely in the water, never venturing on to land. Despite this, it still has not had time to develop (through evolution) underwater breathing apparatus, so every hour or so it must head to the surface to gulp down some air (**note - This is just a turn of phrase - snakes obviously don't "gulp"!*). Contributing to the long period of time that this snake can spend submerged is the fact that it is also able to absorb a little oxygen from the water through its skin.

- Like many other sea snakes, the Dubois Sea Snake has a gland under its tongue which is uses to excrete excess salt from its system.
- During mating, the male and female snake cannot "disengage" *(* note - this is the least evocative word I could come up with here to spare people from imagining this scene in too much detail)* from each other until insemination is complete. Unsurprisingly, *coitus interruptus* is not seen as a viable family planning strategy within this species.

Hook-nosed Sea Snake (*Enhydrina schistosa*)

While the Dubois Sea Snake has more potent venom, the Hook-nosed Sea Snake (sometimes called the Beaked Sea Snake) is involved is many more attacks on humans - by some accounts more than 90% of all sea snake fatalities. This is possibly due to the more aggressive nature of this snake compared to similarly dangerous sea snakes. As is the case with almost all sea snake envenomations, the majority of all attacks on humans by the Hook-nosed Sea Snake come when they become tangled in fishermen's nets.

The Hook-nosed Sea Snake is found in the waters off India, Thailand and Burma, along with a population in the Arabian Sea and the Persian Gulf.

Did you know?

- Its name comes from the distinctive beak-like protrusion sticking out from its nose
- Due to variations between tests, the impressive potency of the venom produced by this snake sees it occasionally listed as possessing the most

potent venom of any snake, with potency as high as 0.02mg/kg being recorded. However, based on the most reliable results we have, the Hook-nosed Sea Snake's neurotoxic and myotoxic venom appears to sit somewhere between the Coastal Taipan and the Forest Cobra in terms of sheer brute strength.

Yellow Bellied Sea Snake (*Pelamis platurus*)

The Yellow Bellied Sea Snake is another sea snake which possesses highly toxic venom, yet poses minimal risk to humans. Despite being the most common (in terms of its wide area of distribution around the Pacific region and some parts of the Indian Ocean) sea snake, it tends to spend most of its time out to sea, away from people. It is 100% aquatic - never emerging from the ocean to sample all that land-based living has to offer.

The Yellow Bellied Sea Snake is easily identified due to its (you may want to sit down before you read this next bit, to avoid undue shock) distinctive yellow undercarriage. This bright yellow colour appears to signal to potential predators that this snake is toxic. Possibly as a consequence (or for reasons as yet unidentified), the snake has no predators.

Like other venomous sea snakes, the Yellow Bellied Sea Snake is highly unlikely to either come into contact with, or bite, a human. However, for anyone unlucky enough to be bitten, the Yellow Bellied Sea Snake possesses extremely potent (mainly neurotoxic) venom. Because of their comparatively small fangs and lack of localised swelling, a person may not even realise they have been bitten. One of the first signs is often drooping eyelids. Without appropriate treatment, this can then progress to full-body paralysis and death.

Did you know?

- The Yellow Bellied Sea Snake appears to be the "Brussels sprouts" of the oceans. Nothing wants to eat this snake. In fact, when scientists skinned a Yellow Bellied Sea Snake and tried feeding it to fish, most refused to even touch it - suggesting that the aversion to eating this snake may not be caused by the yellow coloration. Those fish foolhardy enough to take a mouthful of sweet, sweet Yellow Bellied Sea Snake, promptly hurled it back up again.
- Scientists recently found that the Yellow Bellied Sea Snake is unable to process salt water as per the gland under the tongue associated more generally with sea snakes as a group. Instead, after much observation, they found that these snakes drink rainwater as it lands on the surface of the ocean. This means that a long period of no rain can possibly cause serious dehydration in these snakes.

Tiger Snake (genus *Notechis*)

Yet another Australian snake in possession of brutally powerful venom is the Tiger Snake. There are actually a few members of the genus *notechis*, with the Mainland Tiger Snake (or Common Tiger Snake - *notechis scutatus*) being the most widely known.

Despite their vaguely scary tiger-like markings, this is another fairly shy and reclusive snake in the mould of the Inland Taipan. Tiger Snakes can be an almost "Jekyll & Hyde" species as, while they are generally shy and will avoid conflict if possible; when threatened or cornered they can become extremely aggressive and dangerous. However, unless you step on one, they will almost never attack. I have seen people on nature documentaries handling them and they will almost never bite. I think their name may contribute to the discrepancies between their reputation and reality.

Due to their previous ubiquity around southern Australia, they were until recently the leading causes of snakebite deaths in the country. They have now lost this title to the Eastern Brown, as Tiger Snake numbers have been steadily decreasing as humans encroach on their natural habitat.

The Tiger Snake's potent venom contains a mixture of neurotoxins, myotoxins and hemotoxins. As with other hemotoxic snake bites, the tell-tale sign that the Tiger Snake's bite is hemotoxic is the fact that it can be incredibly painful, with significant swelling at the site of the bite.

Did you know?

- If you are walking through Australian bushland and suddenly all the birds start going crazy, it is a possible indication that there is a Tiger Snake nearby. Tiger Snakes love climbing trees looking for eggs and baby chicks.
- Due to their love of wetlands and small creeks, the Tiger Snake's decreasing numbers may also be linked to climate change, as Australia becomes increasingly dry and drought-prone.

Belcher's Sea Snake (*Hydrophis belcheri*)

No topic is able to send a budding herpetologist's* pulse racing like the controversy surrounding the Belcher's Sea Snake's venom toxicity. The internet is literally full of sites debating whether the Inland Taipan possesses the most toxic venom or whether it is indeed the Belcher's Sea Snake that should rightfully claim that honour.

The problem lies both with the fact that there is a conspicuous absence of verified scientific data on the Belcher's venom and the data that does exist being extremely variable.

Little is known of the Belcher's Sea Snake (sometimes referred to as the Faint Banded Sea Snake) apart from the fact that it is found around Central and South-East Asia along with northern parts of Australia. The lack of information therefore makes this entry rather boring, unless I make some outlandish claim to spice things up. Did you know that researchers have trained a Belcher's Sea Snake to correctly point to the number "4" when asked by trainers "what 2 + 2 equals"?

Did you know?

- The Belcher's Sea Snake is famously mild-mannered. You would literally need to pick it up, crack it like a whip and make disparaging references to its tiny fangs and puny venom yield before it would be interested in biting you. This is perhaps another reason why it doesn't really deserve its place on any "most dangerous" list that you may encounter.

- It is known as the "Belcher's" Sea Snake due to its notorious intolerance of carbonated beverages. Actually, I may have made that up also. Sorry, I need to spice up this entry due to a lack of confirmed facts on this snake. It is actually names after British explorer Sir Edward Belcher.

Someone who studies reptiles - no, not the name for the doctor you need to visit after dodgy Kontiki tour.

Spiders

In the course of researching for this book, if there was one fact I discovered that surprised me more than anything else it was the fact that spiders, on the whole, are not particularly dangerous to human beings. The image that many of us have of spiders - that they are mindless, furry, creepy-crawly killing machines, does not quite align with reality. But I may be biased. Some people are scared of snakes. Personally I have always found spiders much more terrifying. The Sydney Funnel Web in particular looks like something out of my nightmares.

However, if you look at the hard facts, you realise that all but three spiders (or possibly one or two more that can cause some discomfort if they bite you) are perfectly harmless, gentle creatures (OK, maybe not "gentle" per se - I guess there is the whole "liquifying the insides of other insects and sucking them dry" issue). Each year, spiders kill almost no-one.

Like snakes, there is also considerable debate as to which spider should be considered the deadliest. Of the three main, commonly accepted deadly types of spider (Brazilian Wandering Spider, Sydney Funnel Web Spider and the two *latrodectus* varieties - the Black Widow and the Redback) it appears as if the Brazilian Wandering Spider just has the edge over the Sydney Funnel Web in terms of venom potency. However, there are also claims that both of these spiders' venoms are dwarfed in potency by the obscure Six-eyed Sand Spider. By all accounts, if you are unlucky enough to be bitten by one of these things, you will be begging for death to claim you post-haste.

In terms of deaths, the Black Widow is the clear front runner. However even this spider is responsible for less than 50 deaths since records began. To put that in perspective, the Saw-Scaled Viper kills around 50,000 people per annum. To reiterate - spiders are not particularly deserving of their fearsome reputation.

However if we pull out further to take in the full arachnid class, we find a different story. If you are telling the story of deadly arachnids, you can essentially ignore the spiders altogether due to their significantly more dangerous cousin - the scorpion! (Cue dramatic music and close-up). Scorpions are believed to be responsible for more than a million attacks each year that lead to more than 3,000 fatalities. More than one thousand people die from scorpion sting each year in Mexico alone!

One spider that does not quite qualify as "deadly" but deserves an honourable mention is the Brown Recluse Spider (*Loxosceles reclusa*), who's bite can lead to tissue literally rotting away. If you have a strong stomach, you will be able to find pictures on the internet to see firsthand the gut-churning effects of this spider's bite. If you are bitten by this spider you probably won't die, but you may no longer draw admiring glances from the opposite sex when you hit the beach on account of you having large chunks of your arm or leg missing.

One last honourable mention should go to the little-known distant relative of the Brown Recluse that goes by the highly imaginative name of the Six-Eyed Sand Spider (*Sicarius hahni*) which is found in the deserts of Africa. Some experts are of the opinion that this unassuming character possesses the most toxic venom of any spider. The venom in question is powerfully cytotoxic, virtually killing any cell it comes into contact with. The other bad news is that as of now, no antivenin exists. The good news, however, is that as well as spending its time far away from humans, it appears to be exceedingly reluctant to bite people. There are only a handful of suspected envenomations and even these are not confirmed. However in one of these cases, the person's arm near rotted off due to tissue necrosis - perhaps a good indication that this spider may have been involved.

Sydney Funnel Web (*Atrax robustus*)

Being Australian, I may be biased, however by far the spider that I find the most terrifying is the Sydney Funnel Web. To me they look like the prototypical "scary spider". They are a murderous, murderous looking spider. Sorry, I am getting carried away already. Anyway, suffice to say, they are murderous. End of story.

On paper, the Sydney Funnel Web has a lot in common with the Brazilian Wandering Spider. Both have highly potent neurotoxic venom with fairly similar LD50 numbers and neither have killed anyone since the development of antivenin.

Unlike most other spiders, it is actually the males that cause the most problems due to their habit of wandering around looking for females to mate with. There is only one thing creepier than males out on the town looking for a female to hook up with - if that male is actually a murderous, murderous Sydney Funnel Web. Not only are you exceedingly unlikely to come into contact with a female Funnel Web, their venom is also considerably less potent.

So, now on to the horrors of an actual attack. The initial bite will most likely be excruciatingly painful due to both the large punctures in your skin made by the large fangs but also the acid pH of the venom. Did you just make a little scared squeak like I did when I first read this?

Yes, large puncture marks. From Sydney Funnel Web fangs. But it gets better! In some cases, due to the large puncture made in the skin, the spider gets (wait for it) - stuck to your body! I literally start to try to visualise what this would be like but need to pull back, lest I traumatise myself. So, you are in agony, running around in circles trying to dislodge one of the most venomous (and possibly the most murderous) creatures in the world off your person. The only possible way to garnish this scene would be if it was stuck to your face. I would literally just turn to stone, like a kind of petrified tree.

If you are able to get past this initial attack without taking your own life, you then have agonising cramps and possible coma to look forward to.

Thank god for antivenin is all I can say.

Did you know?

- If Fluffy the cat or Patch the dog get bitten by a Funnel Web you can expect…nothing to happen. Many animals such as cats and dogs are immune to the Funnel Web's venom. Unfortunately, for whatever reason, it appears that primates (including humans) are particularly vulnerable to these spiders. Lucky us.
- The average male Funnel Web stores around 8mg of venom in their body and uses around 2mg in the average envenomation. Of this, 0.1mg is enough to kill a human if they do not receive antivenin.
- You will notice that quite often in this book I will mention how shy and retiring a particular animal is. How it is unfairly labelled a "killer". Not the Sydney Funnel Web. Nasty, nasty, aggressive spider (well, the males at least). One minute you are minding your business wandering around Sydney and the next minute you have a big black spider stuck to your face, laying eggs in your mouth*
- Fortunately, these spiders are only found in a 100km radius around the Australian city of Sydney. If you are afraid of deadly creatures, you may want to give Sydney (and the rest of Australia for that matter) a wide berth. Want to head further inland to escape the Funnel Web? You have the Inland Taipan and the Eastern Brown waiting for you.

Quick, jump in the ocean! I hear you say. There you have Great White Sharks, Bull Sharks and Box Jellyfish to contend with. If you are looking for a holiday free of deadly animals, I recommend you look elsewhere.

- Funnel Web Spiders can't climb up smooth surfaces, so if, for some reason, you have one in a jar, there is no need to put a lid on.

* Note - I have no actual proof that they will lay eggs in your mouth. This is pure conjecture at this point.

Brazilian Wandering Spider (*Phoneutria*)

In terms of bragging rights, the Brazilian Wandering Spider can claim the title of "world's deadliest spider" in a photo finish with the Funnel Web. However the differences between the two are completely academic - if either of these spiders bites you (and it's not a dry bite) and you don't get treated soon after, you will stand a reasonable chance of expiring.

The venom of this spider is a fascinating cocktail of various neurotoxic substances that can lead to convulsions, paralysis and then, if left untreated, death.

One thing I find perplexing about this spider is that, despite the fact that it tends to regularly come into contact with humans, deaths have historically been rare. Up until the development of effective antivenin, there have only been 16 recorded deaths attributed to it. Fortunately, since then there have been no further deaths. One of the explanations for this is the fact that Brazilian Wandering Spider species (there are several sub-species in this group) dry-bite around two-thirds of the time. They appear to value their venom and only use it sparingly. Another possible cause for the low number of deaths is the propensity of this spider to give fair warning before it bites. When threatened it will rear up to warn off anything that disturbs it. I have seen vision of this display and it would not only dissuade me from harassing it but would also cause my lower intestine to loosen ever so slightly.

Brazilian Wandering Spiders (whose official name means "murderess" in Latin - as if you needed no further indication of its potential to cause you injury) are named as such due to the fact that they tend to wander around the forest looking for prey, rather than using a web to ensnare their victims.

Did you know?

- The Brazilian Wandering Spider venom is being studied by scientists as a potential treatment for erectile dysfunction as a bite from this spider can cause priapism in males. Priapism is essentially an unwanted erection that lasts for hours. *Fun times!* I hear you say. Not quite. In extreme cases, priapism needs to be treated by inserting a syringe into the penis to deflate it like a balloon. Go on, look it up - I swear I am not making this up. Since reading this I have placed priapism at Number 3 in my list of "things I never want to happen to me". Number 2 involves a Sydney Funnel Web and Number 1 involves an Andre Rieu concert.
- The tendency of this spider to hang out in bunches of bananas has seen a few reports of them turning up in other parts of the world, with generally unfavourable reception. Recently a British couple found their bunch of bananas purchased from the local grocer was infested with hundreds of Brazilian Wandering Spiders. I smell a refund and potentially some gift cards in their future.

The Black Widow (*Latrodectus mactans*) & The Redback (*Latrodectus hasseltii*)

As we have seen in the section on venomous snakes, the dangerousness of a particular creature is only weakly linked to the LD50 value of its venom. Better indicators of potential fatalities are - tendency to live around humans and being located in a third-world country with poor access to antivenin. Put another way, once an animal has passed a certain minimum threshold required to be able to kill a human, it is more important where they are located, rather than increased potency of venom. The venom of the latrodectus species is hundreds of times weaker than, say, a Geographic Cone Snail, yet these spiders have killed many more people.

Spiders in the latrodectus genus certainly tick the box in terms of living around humans. My experience with Redbacks has been that they appear to preferentially target man-made objects to hide in, over natural structures like trees or fallen logs. It is this tendency to invade man-made areas that has led to the 36 confirmed deaths in the US since 1965. This death toll would be significantly higher if they were concentrated in Africa or South East Asia.

Whilst the venom of latrodectus is reasonably potent (the venom contains a cocktail of neurotoxic chemicals, with the main component known as *latrotoxin*), another saving grace is the fact that these spiders can only deliver around 2mgs each time they bite you. By way of comparison, the Russel's Viper has similarly potent venom, but delivers ninety times as much venom each time it bites you! Consequently, nowadays it is really only small children, the old and the infirm that are at any risk from a latrodectus bite.

In general, if you are bitten by any of the latrodectus species, you can expect intense pain and just a hint of violent vomiting, but death would be unlikely.

There are a range of Black Widow species however in general, when we refer to a Black Widow we are talking about the Southern Black Widow (*latrodectus mactans*). The Black Widow earned its name due to the habit that female Black Widows have of eating the males after mating. Not only do I not understand the evolutionary sense of this (doesn't it deter males at all?), but it also makes for strained post-coital banter between the two spiders (The worst possible thing a male Black Widow can hear from the female after mating is *"Does my abdomen look big in this?"*). Mating is done the good old fashioned way - When two spiders develop romantic feelings for each other, the male spider will gently insert his palpus into the female spider's spermathecal opening.*

Australians are terrorised by their own latrodectus species - *latrodectus hasseltii*, or the Redback Spider. In Australia, Redbacks are ubiquitous, posing a much greater risk of envenomation (in terms of frequency) than the more deadly Funnel Web Spider.

Did you know?

- Recently, scientists worked out that male Black Widows will preferentially mate with females that are well-fed - indicating that they do not just resign themselves to inevitable post-coital demise. The male appears to be able to sense chemical signals from the female that indicates she is not hungry and is therefore less likely to eat him. Where this gets really interesting however, is when we look at the Redback's mating habits. Male Redbacks appear to actually want to get eaten after mating. After he has finished his business and pulled his palpus out of her spermathecal opening**, he will often crawl around the female and place himself in front of her mouthparts. Here is where evolution is clearer. A female Redback that has recently eaten her male lover is less likely to entertain subsequent gentlemen callers. Also, there may be a desire on his part to get his cute little spiderlings off to the best possible start, nutrition wise.

- Due to their habit of hiding under toilet seats, one of the most common places to be bitten is on the buttocks or genitals. As a result, I have not been able to identify a single case where a friend or loved-one has offered to suck the poison out.***

* Note - If you just got a little turned on reading this, you may need professional help.

** - Note - Gratuitous use of the terms "palpus" and "spermathecal opening".

*** Note - This is a bad joke. You should never suck the poison out in any cases of envenomation.

Scorpions

    As I mentioned earlier, as a group, scorpions are by far the most deadly group of arachnids, killing thousands every year in various parts of the globe. Due to the fact that the majority of all deaths occur in third world countries, obtain an exact annual death toll is difficult. I have seen figures as low as 3000 annual deaths and as high as 30,000 deaths per year in India alone.

    The other problem we have in assessing the toxicity of scorpion venom is that there are many different scorpion families, ranging from harmless to deadly. And even within a single genus there is enormous variability in toxicity of venom. Scorpion venom is notoriously heterogenous, making any blanket assessment of toxicity rather difficult. For example, scorpion venom can contain a mix of neurotoxins, cardiotoxins, nephrotoxins (toxic for the kidneys) along with a range of other substances such as various enzymes, histamine and serotonin (serotonin in bites causes intense pain). The most significant of these are the neurotoxins which trigger a massive release of stress hormones such as norepinephrine (noradrenaline). This is why a victim's blood pressure and heart rate can skyrocket.

    General consensus is that some of the most deadly scorpions include the Indian Red Scorpion, the Fat-Tailed Scorpion and the ominously named Deathstalker Scorpion. All of these more deadly scorpions have venom that compares favourably with the deadliest of snakes, albeit at lower yield (the scorpion's stinger doesn't quite have the same ability as a snake's fangs in terms of delivering large quantities of venom into a human).

When hunting and capturing prey (as opposed to stinging humans in self-defence), the scorpion will hold the unfortunate creature in its pincers while stabbing it with its tail, injecting venom to immobilise and kill it.

Did you know?

- Many scorpions have evolved in harsh, unforgiving environments such as arid deserts where food and water is scarce. Consequently they have developed impressive control over their own metabolism to the point where, if there is a lack of food, they can get by on as little as one insect per year.
- Further adding to their formidable reputation as hardy creatures, many scorpions can be frozen solid and thawed out, only to dust themselves off and walk away as if nothing happened.
- Due to substances in their exoskeletons, many scorpions glow in the dark (particularly under fluorescent black lighting)
- There is an animal called a Grasshopper Mouse that is immune to scorpion venom. As this particular mouse eats scorpions, over millions of years it appears to have evolved a special protection that prevents it from feeling any pain when stung by a scorpion. In other animals, scorpion venom stimulates the sodium channels that are involved in the transmission of pain. In the Grasshopper Mouse, the venom has the exact opposite effect - it blocks these channels. Scorpion venom is like morphine for these mice!

Sea Creatures

Geographic Cone Snail (*Conus Geographus*)

I know what you're thinking - I spent my hard-earned cash on this cockamamie book, only to be told that a snail possesses the most potent venom known to man? Hopefully I can make it up to you by explaining the reason they possess such powerful venom, which is actually quite interesting. Before I tell you, have a quick think as to why a cone snail would evolve venom with such potency.

These slow moving snails hunt fast moving fish, so when they get the chance to envenomate and immobilise prey, they need to make sure they do it properly, or the fish will swim off and die somewhere far away, to be eaten by some other lucky creature.

The Geographic Cone Snail lives in a (prepare to be shocked to your very core) cone-shaped shell, on the shallow reefs of the Pacific and Indian oceans. It hunts by shooting a harpoon-like proboscis into its prey (or a hapless human), injecting the target with an unimaginably powerful cocktail of toxins. For a small animal such as a fish, due to the power of the venom, it will have enough time to say *"Tell my wife and kids I..."* before it promptly falls dead (or sinks dead, as the case may be).

Due to the much larger body mass of a human, we have more of a chance of surviving, as the snail injects only a tiny amount of venom compared to say, a cobra. Interestingly, whilst the sting is initially excruciating, everything soon becomes numb, as the venom has a super-potent analgesic as part of the cocktail (more on this in a moment). Soon after, as the neurotoxic venom (known as *conotoxin*) goes to work, you will start to experience all the symptoms consistent with other neurotoxic venoms - drooping eyelids, tingling, blurred vision, difficulty speaking and the like. Amazingly, because of the lack of an effective antivenin and how quick the venom takes hold, there is little anyone can do except try to keep you breathing and wait to see if you will die during the critical 1-5 hour window.

Did you know?

- The Cone Snail eats its prey (small fish) whole and then later, regurgitates the bones.
- Due to the powerful analgesic (painkiller) contained in the venom, it is being studied as a potential alternative to morphine for those suffering from severe pain. Naturally, the analgesic component needs to be isolated to ensure people aren't subjected to the neurotoxic substances in the venom - you can't just grab a Cone Snail and suck some venom out of its proboscis (at least without asking it first) when you have a headache.
- There is no safe way to handle a Cone Snail in your hand, as they can harpoon you from any angle. This has made the task of "milking" them (to extract the venom) difficult for researchers looking at potential medicinal applications. At this stage, the only way to isolate the venom is to tempt the snail with a fish so that it injects it with venom, before they then extract the venom from the fish.

Blue-Ringed Octopus (*Hapalochlaena*)

What does a Blue-Ringed Octopus and a Pufferfish have in common?

They both possess a type of toxin known as *tetrodotoxin*, a neurotoxin 1000 times more potent than cyanide. Tetrodotoxin works on your sodium channels, inhibiting the firing of certain neurons, leading to paralysis of your diaphragm and consequently, death from asphyxiation.

The first sign that you have been poisoned or envenomated with tetrodotoxin is usually various paraesthesia (abnormal sensations like buzzing, prickling or numbness of the skin). In Japan, when you consume *fugu* (Pufferfish), if the chef has not removed all the tetrodotoxin, your best case scenario is numbness around the lips and your worst case scenario is death. In Japan, as healthcare has improved (and possibly the know-how of chefs preparing this dish) the number of annual fatalities has been dropping over time. In recent years, less than five people have died each year (with many more non-fatal poisonings), whereas half a century ago, the death toll would occasionally reach almost two hundred in some years. (More on this soon in the section on Pufferfish)

Similarly to snakes, the Blue-Ringed Octopus produces its own supply of tetrodotoxin in modified saliva glands. If you are unlucky enough to be envenomated by one of these diminutive cephalopods you will be faced with the unfortunate fact that there is no known treatment for tetrodotoxin poisoning. The good news is that if you survive the first 24 hours, you will most likely be out of the woods. Due to the fact that a bite from a Blue-Ringed Octopus can cause respiratory failure, this is one of the few cases where mouth-to-mouth resuscitation is still recommended. If someone you are with is attacked, you may literally have to breathe for your friend to keep them alive.

Unfortunately, in their habitat around the shallows of Australia and other parts of the Indo-Pacific, they tend to congregate in areas frequented by beach-goers, leading to several attacks and occasional fatalities each year.

I may be stating the obvious here, however if you are poking around a tidal rock pool in Australia and have yet to be eaten by a Great White Shark or stung by a Box Jellyfish and you see an adorable little octopus with just the cutest little blue rings, take a moment to pause. Use your powers of deduction to put two and two together - it's an octopus and it has blue rings. Even if there is still an element of doubt remaining, I would exercise caution, turn around and head in the opposite direction. Except, don't step on that rock that just moved. It's a Stonefish and will also kill you. Maybe just head straight back to the airport.

Did you know?

- The Blue-Ringed Octopus injects its venom via a small beak on its underside. This is the most common question people have regarding these creatures, as the beak is relatively hidden and not immediately obvious.
- Due to the fact that a Blue-Ringed Octopus bite can cause paralysis, some people report that they are completely conscious but frozen inside their body. If this happens to someone you are not particularly fond of, prop them up in front of a TV and make them watch Big Momma's

House, Battlefield Earth or that movie Justin Bieber was in.*

- After they have finished mating, males promptly die, taking the concept of *la petite mort* one step too far. According to some scientists, this apparently puts a lot of pressure on the female octopus.

* Note - You do realise I am joking right? Sorry, I had to check. I don't want any lawsuits from anyone subjected against their will to any Martin Lawrence movie. Also, to the Church of Scientology - this is a comment regarding the 2000 John Travolta movie, not anything directed at Scientology directly. Please do not sue me as I have few assets apart from a 2006 Mitsubishi Outlander with around 50,000 km on the clock.

Stonefish (*Synanceia*)

First, let's deal with the elephant in the room as I don't want to tip-toe around the issue - the Stonefish is one of the most unfortunate looking creatures on God's green earth. Possibly pipped at the post only by some of those deep-sea fish that look like they are ripped straight from a horror movie.

Secondly, due to the fact that I live in Stonefish territory, I am particularly petrified of them. This is due to two reasons. First, as they are notoriously hard to spot, whenever I am walking around reefs or even in the water and I step on something sharp, immediately I start to plan the quickest route to a spot on the beach where an ambulance can get quick access to my convulsing body. Secondly, being stung by a Stonefish when you step on them is apparently one of the most painful experiences a human can endure - eclipsed only by watching the dressage or anything remotely equestrian at the Olympics. Once the ambulance arrives, grab the paramedic by the shirt-sleeves and demand IV morphine. In terms of dose, ask them to find the sweet-spot just before death from respiratory failure. This is no time to scrimp on the morphine.

The Stonefish delivers its venom via dorsal spines that are in just the right spot to spike a foot. Herein lies my main beef with the

Stonefish - If you have taken the time over millions of years to evolve these spikes on your back to avoid getting trodden on, WHY HAVE YOU ALSO EVOLVED TO LOOK LIKE A ROCK THAT NO-ONE HAS A CHANCE OF NOTICING? Sorry, as you can see Stonefish get me a little riled.

Stonefish venom is still rather mysterious in terms of mechanism of action, however researchers believe it primarily acts as a neurotoxin, with secondary action as a cytotoxin and myotoxin.

Did you know?

- Stonefish can stay out of the water for more than 24 hours!
- The Stonefish envenomation can be so painful that victims have been known to either demand to be euthanized or have the affected limb amputated.
- Stonefish venom is believed to be similar to Black Widow venom, albeit at much higher potency and (probably) amount injected.
- In the same family as the Stonefish are the equally ghastly, if not slightly less dangerous Scorpionfish and Lionfish.

Box Jellyfish (*Cubozoa*)

     Another delight of the beguiling Australian oceanic landscape is the class of jellyfish known as the Box Jellyfish. However, usually when you hear someone refer to *"...those f*****g box jellyfish..."* they are referring to either Chironex Fleckeri (the Sea Wasp), Malo Kingi (the Irukandji) or Carukia Barnesi (also known as the Irukandji - I will get to this in a moment).

     Let's look at the Sea Wasp first. Some of the creatures in this book, whilst theoretically "deadly", don't actually kill too many people. Not the Sea Wasp - it's extinguished the promising lives of more than 60 people (on record - many more were killed prior to records beginning or in indigenous tribes where no records are kept). *No problem*, I hear you say, *just get some antivenin in you and you will be home in time for dinner*. Wrong. In cases where someone has become hopelessly entangled in the Sea Wasp's tentacles, death has occurred in as little as three minutes! This seemingly massive over-specified system of envenomation leads to a natural question - Why does a creature who preys on small fish need enough venom to kill 60 grown men? This is probably related to the Geographic Cone Snail's similar situation - a jellyfish is unable to chase down a wounded fish so they literally need to stop their prey dead in its tracks (literally). Another reason would be the fact that jellyfish are quite delicate - a prolonged struggle with a fish in its death-throes could inflict significant damage. Evolution really is fascinating. Over millions of years, the jellyfish with the stronger venom were more likely to survive, leading to our current situation now where they are frighteningly dangerous.

The Sea Wasp (and the other related Box Jellyfish) inject venom via small harpoons on their tentacles, called *cnidocytes* (or *nematocytes*). If a tentacles wraps itself around your arm, these small harpoons all fire, piercing your skin and injecting often large amounts of venom.

Like the Stonefish, the sting of the Sea Wasp is thought to be one of the most painful experiences someone can endure. Based on reports from victims, most people would prefer to give birth to a cactus than to be stung by one of these delightful creatures. Most described the sensation as feeling like they are being branded with a hot poker. The most dangerous scenario is being stung while on your own in deeper waters. Due to the speed with which the venom can take hold, many people have experienced cardiac arrest and drowned on the spot.

Fortunately, in areas with known population of Sea Wasps, there is wide availability of antivenin, however time is still of the essence. If someone is stung, it is incredibly important to get help as soon as possible.

The Sea Wasp is concentrated in the oceans around (wait for it - prepare to be shocked) Australia.

Another type of jellyfish terrorising Australian waters is the Irukandji. The naming can get a little confusing as there are actually two jellyfish known as Irukandji - Malo Kingi and Carukia Barnesi. The reason for this confusing state of affairs is because these two jellyfish are so mysterious, it took a while to identify which creatures were actually inflicting such agony on people unfortunate enough to be stung. These two jellyfish are lumped together because both cause an unpleasant reaction called Irukandji syndrome (named after the Irukandji aborigines of north-eastern Australia).

So, why is this bringer of death so mysterious? Irukandji jellyfish are only around 1cm in size! So you can forget about taking extra care to avoid them. You literally have no chance of knowing if one is right next to you.

A good gauge of how powerful and painful a sting is for a person is the fact that the most potent opiates known are recommended for relieving the pain. The reason for this is due to the fact that such large amounts of painkillers are needed to take the edge off, unless you use the most powerful opiates, you run the risk of dying from overdose (due to respiratory depression) before the pain is ameliorated.

The fact that they are virtually invisible make identification difficult. If you are enjoying a relaxing swim in the tropical waters off Australia, minding your own business, and suddenly you feel more pain than you have ever felt in your life (to the point where suicide is becoming increasingly attractive), this may be an indication that you have been stung by an Irukandji jellyfish. However, the fun doesn't end there. Another delightful effect of the venom is that it has the ability to induce fear and panic. Victims describe it as a feeling of intense impending doom.

Did you know?

- Vinegar stops the cnidocytes from firing into the skin. So if a victim has a Box Jellyfish tentacle still attached to them, this could be the difference between life and death. When someone is initially stung, there will typically be many of the little harpoons that have not yet fired. Trying to remove the tentacle or applying compression will activate the cnidocytes, making the problem worse. If you are swimming in known Box Jellyfish hot-spots, it is recommended to have a bottle of vinegar with you.
- Because the cnidocytes react to chemicals on our skin, wearing women's pantyhose stops them from activating if you come into contact with a Box Jellyfish. As if I didn't need another excuse to wear pantyhose while frolicking in the ocean.

- Certain sea turtles are immune to the sting (or more specifically, the stingers cannot penetrate the shell or skin) and love nothing better than to hunt down and eat Box Jellyfish. I have never loved turtles more than I do right now.
- Box Jellyfish are one of the few jellyfish that can actually swim. Most jellyfish just drift, passively.

Salt Water Crocodile (*Crocodylus porosus*)

　　If I had a choice between being dropped into a tank with a Great White Shark or a Saltwater Crocodile, I would choose the Great White any day of the week. Contrary to popular belief, being in the water with a Great White is not guaranteed death. Whether they attack or not depends on a variety of factors, with hunger being a key determinant. A Saltwater Crocodile is another proposition entirely because they are known as *hyper-aggressive predators*. This essentially means they will kill anything within reach, irrespective of hunger levels.

　　Salt Water crocs are like living dinosaurs, with the earliest specimens dated almost 5 million years ago. By comparison, humans (as *Homo sapiens*) first appeared around 200,000 years ago. Their long reign on the planet is a good indication of their evolutionary toughness. If you had a crocodile on one hand and a dodo on the other, I think I would have a good idea which one will avoid extinction for the longest time. Despite this, since the spread of humans around the globe, Salt Water Crocodiles have disappeared from many parts of Asia, such as Thailand and the Mekong Delta. Fortunately (or unfortunately, depending on your point of view) there is still a large population thriving in (surprise, surprise) Australia. If you decide to take a swim amongst mangroves or tidal swamps in the northern parts of Australia, you stand a not insignificant chance of being devoured.

Conservative estimates put the annual death toll in Australia at around 2-4 people. The most commonly attacked are aborigines or tourists who are not familiar with the risks. One of the more notable of these (in terms of media coverage) was the 2002 fatal attack on German student Isabel von Jordan in Kakadu National Park.

Probably the most famous aspect of a crocodile attack is the death roll, where the crocodile rolls over and over, with the intention of drowning the victim and sometimes tearing limbs off torsos. By all accounts, if you are grabbed by a crocodile, as soon as possible, try to get a finger in its eyes or any other potentially vulnerable spot. Crocodiles aren't used to prey fighting back and have been known to let go of a person after they have poked it in the eye. The worst thing you can do is just struggle, trying to get free. If a crocodile senses you are struggling and may escape, it will take you into the death role. In terms of your prospects for survival, this should not be viewed as a positive development and should be avoided where possible.

Did you know?

- Saltwater Crocodiles have the most powerful bite of any creature on the planet.
- Around 70-80 million years ago there was an ancestor of current day Salt Water Crocs that was known as *Deinosuchus*. This delightful specimen grew as large as 11 metres, making it quite the nightmarish killing machine. Deinosuchus is estimated to have had a more powerful bite force than Tyrannosaurus Rex.
- If we are to define the "deadliest" crocodile in terms of human death toll, the smaller Nile crocodile would be the clear winner by a large margin. A huge population of people share territory with the Nile crocodile, leading to an estimated 200-400 fatalities every year.

Komodo Dragon (*Varanus komodoensis*)

Along with crocodiles, more than any other type of creature, when you look at a Komodo Dragon you get the sense that it belongs more to the time of the dinosaurs instead of modern day. Its overall look and style of locomotion are reminiscent of CGI renderings of herbivorous dinosaurs like Triceratops or Stegosaurus. With one major difference. If you look closely you will notice that the Komodo Dragon possesses prominent, sharp teeth which you would be unlikely to find on any herbivore.

The Komodo Dragon is so-called due to the fact that it is only found on several Indonesian islands, including the largest population on the island of Komodo. The Dragon, which is the largest lizard on earth, can grow as long as 3 metres and weigh more than 70 kg. There are many aspects of this amazing creature that scientists are struggling to understand, with its size being one hot topic of debate.

The large size of these lizards has been attributed to a fascinating concept known as *island gigantism*, which is the phenomenon where animals living isolated on a large island grow unusually large over time due to a lack of natural predators. The most famous example of this would be the now-extinct Dodo Bird, which lived for millennia in relative safety on the island of Mauritius (humans took care of that by wiping Dodos off the face of the earth in short order). Under the theory of island gigantism, normally if animals grow too large and slow, they will be more easily picked off by predators, limiting how large they grow through evolution. Without these pressures, there is a tendency to increase in size (up to a point) over time.

However there is also a differing view which suggests that the size of Komodo Dragons is due to the fact that they are essentially a reasonably direct link back to the time of the dinosaurs, when lizards were significantly larger than they are now. This theory is backed up by the existence of 3.8 million year-old fossils of Komodo Dragons (at least, animals almost identical to modern day Dragons - suggesting ancestry) which are essentially the same size as current living examples.

The other point of contention surrounding Komodo Dragons is their bite. Researchers have long noted that when an animal is bitten by one of these creatures, within a few days it will succumb to sepsis (an infection that spreads from the bite wound). Researchers found that Komodo Dragon saliva contains a horror-show of nasty bacteria including *E.Coli*. Not only this, but scientists also found that the saliva (which is alluringly described as being "red or rusty-brown" in colour), contains strains of common bacteria that were unusually virulent, flourishing at much quicker rates than normal. However, more recently, a few problems have emerged regarding this explanation as to why animals die soon after being bitten.

Firstly, it has been noted that specimens kept in captivity soon lost their trademark mouth full of putrefying bacteria. This points to the dragon's oral hygiene being co-incidental, rather than central to their means of hunting prey. Some researchers have pointed to the faeces-infested water where animals take shelter after being bitten as a potential cause of the infection and subsequent sepsis.

Another spanner in the works (in terms of elucidating exactly why animals invariably die after being bitten by a Komodo Dragon) is the more recent discovery of venom glands in its mouth. The venom has subsequently been analysed and found to contain a mix of toxic proteins that stop coagulation and cause blood pressure to plummet. Some fractions of the Dragon's venom have been found to be almost as potent as similar proteins in the Inland Taipan's venom. Researchers have found that Komodo Dragons possess the same genes for venom that their distant relatives (the snakes) possess.

While the venom hypothesis is now the leading explanation for why animals die after being bitten by Komodo Dragons, there is still no consensus, with impassioned debate flying back and forth. I have only two things in life I will never do, and one of those things is to stand between two Komodo Dragon experts debating this topic.

Another huge misconception is the long-held idea of Komodo Dragons as aggressive attackers of humans that enter their territory. In most cases, if a human wanders into a Dragon's domain, they will flee. Someone would literally have to corner the lizard or in some other way aggravate it before they would be at risk of being bitten.

Did you know?

- In dramatic contrast to their reputation to having worse oral hygiene than that dodgy old distant uncle you have, Komodo Dragons are actually comparatively fastidious in terms of how they look after their mouth. Firstly, they avoid eating faeces, to the point where they will flap the victims intestines around until all the undigested food is removed. Admittedly, they will then eat the faeces-smeared intestines, but a commendable approach to hygiene nonetheless. Then, after eating, they will obsessively rub their teeth and gums up against various objects to dislodge any remaining food particles.
- In fact, Komodo Dragons have such an aversion to faeces that younger Dragons will sometimes roll in the faeces of dead animals to avoid being eaten by larger, dominant adults (yes, Komodo Dragon eat each other on occasion)
- If Komodo Dragons earned points for their classy behaviour in the example prior, they then lose all respect with this next delightful example of table manners. Remember that competition you would have seen on TV where some godforsaken lump of a man is trying to stuff as much pizza or pie as possible in his mouth in order to win some prize

that will be dwarfed in value by future medical bills? (The good news is you won. The bad news is you no longer have a functioning duodenum). Well, Komodo Dragon's see your eating competition and raise it. If a Komodo Dragon is having particular difficulty fitting an unusually large animal (or part thereof) down its throat, it will sometimes run head-first towards a tree to try pushing the piece of food down! It's the equivalent of a human using a mallet to try to hammer a butternut pumpkin down their throat. Stay classy, Komodo Dragons!

- Komodo Dragons (and other Monitor Lizards), obtain information from the air using a forked tongue not unlike a snake's. As with snakes as well, this tongue grabs scent molecules from the air and deposits them in the Jacobson's Organ in base of the nasal cavity.

- The mating behaviour of the Komodo Dragon is also quite interesting. When a male Komodo Dragon is feeling in the mood for lovin' (cue Barry White or Marvin Gaye song), he will jump on top of a female (as she aggressively tries to fight him off) and while he repels her efforts to free herself, will insert his hemipene into her cloaca. If you are thinking it seems a bit "wham bam thankyou ma'am", you will be pleased to hear that he first spends a while flicking his tongue on various parts of the female's body. Unfortunately, this tongue lashing is not for her benefit. He does this to achieve a hemipene erection so that he might insert it in her cloaca (if there is ever a sentence that I wish I could "unread" it was this one). Sometime later, some adorable little Komodo Dragons will emerge from their eggs. They may or may not then be eaten by either the proud mother or father.

Poison Dart Frog (*Dendrobatidae* family)

The Poison Dart Frog deserves a special place in this book as the only genuine "poisonous" creature, with most of the other creatures erroneously labelled "poisonous", actually "venomous". These frogs are one of the best examples of the near universal concept of *aposematism* - where bright, conspicuous colours are a signal to other animals that they seriously do not want to try eating you (The opposite to aposematism is crypsis, where an animal uses camouflage to stop itself from being eaten). From an evolutionary perspective this naturally makes perfect sense. Poison dart frogs are like those footballers that wear brightly coloured shoes - if you are going to adorn yourself with conspicuous colours, you'd better have the game to back it up. More interesting is the fact that predators seem to have an almost innate aversion to brightly coloured prey.

When we refer to Poison Dart Frogs we are actually referring to the *dendrobatidae* family which contains many different species, some of which are not even toxic. The superstar of the group (in terms of toxicity) is the Golden Poison Frog which is found on the Pacific coast of Colombia. Various native tribes in this part of the world add poison from the Golden Poison Frog to the tips of their arrows - hence the name.

The skin of the Golden Poison Frog (and other poisonous frogs of the same family) is coated in a type of poison known as *batrachotoxin*, which interferes with your body's ability to transmit nerve signals, leading to potential convulsions or cardiac arrest. There is no known antidote or antivenin for batrachotoxin.

Poison Dart Frogs are not naturally poisonous - they produce the toxic alkaloids in their skin from the food they eat. Poison Dart Frogs kept in captivity will often become completely harmless due to the change in diet. However, unfortunately scientists have yet to identify which of the frog's prey is responsible for giving them this amazing ability to produce powerful toxins. Various theories point to either ants or a type of beetle. Giving credence to the beetle theory is the existence of a particular bird that eats beetles similar to those eaten by the Poison Dart Frog and has been found to contain the same toxin (albeit at lower concentrations). What I find most interesting about this, is that it suggests that if the availability of food changes (due to changes in climate, for example), the frogs will be stuck with their confident and festive livery but without the protection of their legendary toxicity. Perhaps, for a while, they will remain untouched by predators due to reputation alone.

Did you know?

- The native tribes that use these frogs for their poison do so by applying heat to the frogs to make them sweat out their precious cargo. Fortunately (or unfortunately - I'm not sure which) the frogs are killed first.
- The Golden Poison Frog's batrachotoxin is around ten times more potent than the tetrodotoxin found in the Pufferfish. However more interesting is the fact that tetrodotoxin is a theoretical antidote to poisoning from

batrachotoxin due to its ability to block the receptor activation caused by this poison. I should point out that this is theoretical - I haven't been able to find anywhere where this was backed up with results from any trials or experiments.

Mosquito

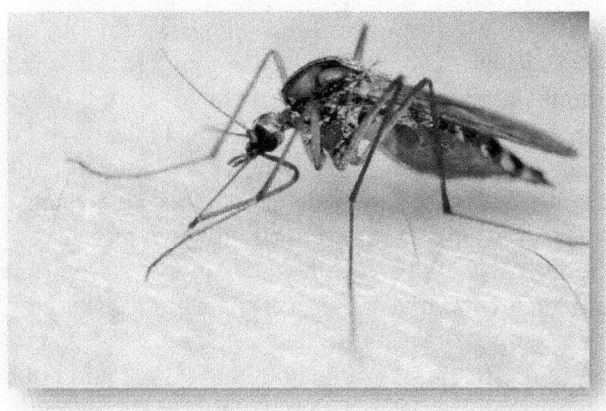

In terms of "deadliness" nothing even comes close to mosquitoes. The only thing that has killed more people, is other people. This is not due to any malice on the mosquito's part - they do not set out to kill people. The tens of millions (if not hundreds of millions, once we go back far enough in history) of deaths are all due to one simple issue - a mosquito drinks blood from one person and then drinks blood from another. So, in practical terms, if a mosquito bites someone with malaria, dengue fever or similar blood-borne disease and then bites another person, it transmits the virus via its proboscis.

According to the World Health Organisation (WHO), mosquitoes kill more than 1 million people each and every year. The majority of deaths are caused by malaria and the majority of all deaths are concentrated in Africa. I was surprised to read that, perhaps stupidly, I had always thought malaria was a virus. However it turns out that it is a parasitic protozoa called plasmodium. If you are infected with this particularly pernicious protozoa, what starts with headache and fever, if left untreated can then progress to coma and death. As with all the other African deaths in this book, quite tragically, malaria is both preventable and treatable.

However it is not just malaria lurking in a mosquito's bag of tricks. It is also responsible for transmitting viruses such as dengue fever (25,000 deaths per annum) and yellow fever (30,000 deaths per annum) across the third world. Mosquitoes are also responsible for the debilitating Ross River Fever, which is also found in Australia - one of the only examples of mosquitoes wreaking havoc on the first world too.

Make no mistake - the mosquito has spread misery and death around our planet for millions of years, however more recently we were spared what could have been an epidemic without precedent. When the HIV virus was identified and started striking down men in the gay community in the early 1980s, a collective shiver went through mankind as we contemplated what may befall us if mosquitoes started transmitting the virus. However, in one of the most fortunate developments in our history, it turned out that HIV could not be transmitted by mosquitoes, who actually digest the virus and do not transmit it when it moves from person to person. Despite this piece of good fortune, tragically, more than a million people still die each year from HIV-related complications. If mosquitoes had added to this, the death toll would have been unimaginable.

Did you know?

- Don't you hate it when, you get stung by a bee and you curse their very existence, only for some tree-hugging communist to unhelpfully point out that without bees, our very existence on earth would be imperilled? It seems that no matter how toxic or unlikable an animal, their extinction will cause a chain reaction that will lead to the earth looking like something out of a Mad Max movie. Not so with mosquitoes apparently. There are some researchers who have studied mosquitoes in depth who have reached the conclusion that complete eradication of mosquitoes from the planet would be unlikely to cause widespread problems. As you may have noticed, in general, no matter how annoying or dangerous a creature, wiping them from the face of the planet will usually lead to undesirable consequences. Perhaps said creature serves as an important food source or fulfils another important role. However in the case of mosquitoes, the majority of animals that feed on mosquitoes have alternative food sources they could turn to if mosquitoes ceased to exist. To be honest, I was completely surprised to read this, as I am previously on record telling my daughter (who has a serious-sounding, yet relatively benign condition called "insect bite hypersensitivity" that involves an exaggerated histamine reaction to mosquito bites) that we have to put up with them because they are needed as a food source. Evidently I was wrong.

- Mosquitoes have a preference for O-type blood. No one is sure why.
- They also appear to have a preference for dark-coloured clothing for some reason. It has been hypothesised that this gives them a degree of protection as they don't stand out as much as when they land on light-coloured surfaces.
- Drinking beer also appears to increase your allure to a prospective mosquito.
- The saliva of a mosquito contains substances that prevent blood clotting, allowing them to feast on your hard-earned blood without risk of getting their proboscis stuck.
- Male mosquitoes do not drink blood. The females use your blood as a food source for growing eggs. Contrary to popular opinion, mosquitoes do not use your blood as their own food source. Adult mosquitoes feast on sugar-rich nectar mostly. As male mosquitoes do not even harm humans, it would be nice if we could just eliminate all the female mosquitoes and leave the males in peace. Oh, hang on, that won't work. Back to the drawing board.
- Apparently if you see a mosquito feeding on your blood, instead of squishing them you can either tense your muscles or stretch the skin around the mosquito taut and kill the mosquito by exploding it. All good in theory however I am yet to meet someone who can just watch a mosquito drinking their blood without squashing it. Plus, exploding a mosquito sounds a little sadistic.
- Mosquitoes can sense the carbon dioxide you exhale from around 30-40 metres away, using it to locate you as a potential meal.
- The reason why mosquitoes are particularly prevalent around still water

is because the females like to deposit eggs into stagnant (and therefore safe for the larvae) water.

- In Canada, a mosquito was found preserved in 80 million year old amber, making them significantly older than humans as a species.
- In another piece of wicked evolutionary development, when a mosquito is infected with the dengue virus, the virus drives them to become insatiable for blood and thereby increasing the chances of transmitting it to others.
- The unbearably itchy red bite mark on your skin is caused by the mosquito's saliva which contains substances that trigger a histamine reaction. This is the reason why antihistamines are so effective at reducing the itch.

Pufferfish (*Tetraodontidae*)

I have no concrete proof however I suspect that, like mosquitoes, if you completely eradicated Pufferfish from the planet, we would be no worse off. Ghastly things.

As any fellow fisherman will know (depending on where you live) these creatures are the bane of our existence. Once hooked that are incredibly hard to unhook without resorting to methods that run the risk of angering the RSPCA or PETA.

Pufferfish have evolved some interesting defences to avoid being eaten. Firstly, when threatened, they inflate themselves into a large spiky ball to dissuade any potential predator from eating them. Then, any animal desperate or dumb enough to actually eat the Pufferfish will find out about the second (and significantly more deadly) line of defence.

The Pufferfish is the second most poisonous (vertebrate) creature on earth (after the Golden Tree Frog) because of a particularly nasty poison it contains, called *tetrodotoxin*. Tetrodotoxin, which you will remember from the Blue Ringed Octopus, is a potent neurotoxin that can paralyse breathing muscles, leading to coma and death.

So, naturally humans stay well away from this unsavoury fish right? Wrong!

In places like Japan, Korea and China, Pufferfish is a delicacy. In Japan (where it is known as *fugu*), they eat Pufferfish in various ways including soups and as raw slices of sashimi. Due to the inherent danger involved, fugu can only be prepared by licensed chefs who undergo extensive training and certification. The poison is concentrated in the liver and ovaries, so preparation involves preventing this poison from contaminating the flesh.

Despite all the precautions, up to six people still die each year from tetrodotoxin poisoning after eating fugu in Japan. It is believed that some of these deaths are actually suicides.

While the majority of the poison is concentrated in the organs of the fish, there is also sometimes a small amount in the flesh. The signs of this mild tetradotoxin poisoning are numb or tingling lips and sometimes mild intoxication. I know this myself as I have experienced this weird sensation after consuming fugu sashimi in Japan. And what did I think of this "delicacy"? To me it just tastes like fish, to be quite honest. Not something I would willingly risk my life to experience. Especially considering the small serving on my table cost around 20,000 yen (around USD$200) (No, I wasn't paying. If I was paying, we would be enjoying a similarly toxic meal at McDonalds)

Did you know?

- The poisonous tetrodotoxin in Pufferfish is produced by bacteria in its gut. Some Japanese fish farmers however, have been able to eliminate the bacteria in question from the Pufferfish diet, thereby producing a completely harmless fish for human consumption.
- It takes more than 3 years of training to become licensed to serve fugu in Japan. The process is so strict and arduous that only around one-third of trainees pass.
- In 1975, a famous kabuki actor with the seriously cool name of *Bandō*

Mitsugorō VIII consumed a generous portion of fugu, claiming to be immune to the poison. He wasn't. He died.

What about creatures whose bite/sting (or however they treat you in some injurious way) is not deadly, but is so painful you may wish you were dead?

Above a certain level of pain, humans tend to make fluid re-evaluations of their usual preference for life over death. The closest I have come was when I had severe food poisoning which lasted for several tortuous days. At various points I remember gazing wistfully at the window next to the bed which I could have jumped out of, into the sweet embrace of death (Or, more likely, some kind of brambly, yet frustratingly cushioned thicket or native scrub growing beneath the window).

Similarly, there are animals with stings so brutish and over the top that unfortunate victims have described death as taking on what, up until that point, had been an unfamiliar degree of appeal. At least when you are bitten by an Eastern Brown you know that, if things get out of hand, you can just promptly expire and be done with the whole thing. Not so with these creatures.

Most of what we know about these kinds of non-deadly yet exceedingly painful creatures is due to the pioneering work of entomologist Justin Schmidt. This brave scientist has even created the eponymous *Schmidt Sting Pain Index*, which ranks the pain from the bites of 78 different creatures. To create this index, Schmidt subjected himself to the bite of each and every one of the creatures covered.

Whilst Schmidt's efforts should be commended, I can't help but feel he stopped short, leaving open a vacancy for someone to take this to the next level. This foolhardy individual (I have no idea who he or she might be. The only thing I know with any degree of certainty is it won't be your humble author) should subject themselves to the bites of each of the venomous creatures in this book, but with antivenin on hand to stave off death. To learn the subjective differences between say, the bite of an Inland Taipan and the bite of a Sydney Funnel Web would be of beguiling interest to myself and many others. Depending on how long the antivenin takes to work, this test subject may even be able to answer some of the bigger questions around life after death, in the event that things take too long and a tunnel of pure light opens up before them. Hopefully the person I speak of is reading this book and now feels they have received my tacit approval to go ahead with this project. Godspeed!

Red Harvester Ant

This ghastly creature haunts the South-West United States, with a particular concentration in Texas, which really didn't need additional reasons for people not to visit. If they feel you are encroaching on their territory or pose a threat to the hive, they will rain down serious hurt on your person. Schmidt said the bite of this ant was *"Bold and unrelenting. Somebody is using a drill to excavate your ingrown toenail"*

Paper Wasp

Actually wasps could potentially be in the "deadly" section also, as many people in Australia have died from anaphylactic shock after being bitten by a wasp.

Paper Wasps aren't as downright belligerent as some other wasps and hornets but they make up for this with their painful bite. Schmidt opined that the bite had a *"Distinctly bitter aftertaste. Like spilling a beaker of hydrochloric acid on a paper cut."* Another brave Aussie who was attacked said that *"...all of a sudden I felt four simultaneous sharp pains, three in my knee and one on the back of my hand. Wow did it hurt! I looked up, I could see five or six wasps all buzzing around me, so I did the sensible thing. I ran away screaming like a little girl, waving my arms around in the air doing an impression of a Chinook helicopter."*

Tarantula Hawk

Tarantula Hawks are a type of wasp so ghastly, they do things to other creatures that shouldn't happen anywhere in the universe, yet clearly do. According to its Wikipedia page, *"The female tarantula hawk captures, stings, and paralyzes the spider, then either drags her prey back into her own burrow or transports it to a specially prepared nest, where a single egg is laid on the spider's abdomen, and the entrance is covered. When the wasp larva hatches, it creates a small hole in the spider's abdomen, then enters and feeds voraciously, avoiding vital organs for as long as possible to keep the spider alive."* That is wrong on so many levels.

According to Schmidt, the bite is *"...Blinding, shockingly electric. A running hair drier has been dropped into your bubble bath."*

Bullet Ant

According to Schmidt, the granddaddy of nasty bites is the Bullet Ant, whose bite he describes as *"Like fire-walking over flaming charcoal with a 3-inch rusty nail grinding into your heel."*

Some Brazilian tribes have a "coming of age" ritual where someone wears a glove full of Bullet Ants. According to many sources, this is the worst pain known to man. Recently, Australian comedy duo Hamish and Andy visited one of these tribes as part of their TV show, whereupon Hamish agreed to put his hand into one of these gloves. It didn't go well. After spending two hours in unbearable pain, eventually Hamish was transported by boat to hospital to so he could be administered potent doses of painkillers, anti-inflammatories and anti-histamines. This is not something I have any ambitions of emulating.

If you enjoyed this book (or at least, don't find yourself openly hostile towards your experience of reading it), please consider leaving a review here on Amazon.

And if you are interested in reading any other books by me, please check out my travel book Naked in a Japanese Hot Spring, which is written under my *Kriece* alias. There is also a fiction book I wrote but it is garbage so I am not going to recommend it.